The Georgia Open History Library has been made possible in part by a major grant from the National Endowment for the Humanities: Democracy demands wisdom. Any views, findings, conclusions, or recommendations expressed in this collection, do not necessarily represent those of the National Endowment for the Humanities.

GENERAL LACHLAN McINTOSH

Lachlan McIntosh Papers in the University of Georgia Libraries

Edited with an Introduction by
LILLA MILLS HAWES

UNIVERSITY OF GEORGIA LIBRARIES
MISCELLANEA PUBLICATIONS, NO. 7

UNIVERSITY OF GEORGIA PRESS
ATHENS   1968

Reissue published in 2021

Most University Press titles are available from popular e-book vendors.

Printed digitally

ISBN 9780820359410 (Hardcover)
ISBN 9780820359403 (Paperback)
ISBN 9780820359397 (Ebook)

Copyright © 1968
University of Georgia Press
Library of Congress Catalog Card Number: 68-22842
Printed in the United States of America

Contents

Foreword to the Reissue	vii
Foreword *by* W. P.	xiii
Kellam Introduction	1

PART I

Letters and Documents	9

PART II

Journals	94
Notes	123
Index	131

Other Publications in the Series

Laws of the Creek Nation
Edited by Antonio J. Waring
No. 1 $1.00

John Howard Payne to His Countrymen
Edited by Clemens de Baillou
No. 2 $2.00

Life and Public Services of an Army Straggler, 1865
By Kittrell J. Warren
Edited by Floyd C. Watkins
No. 3 $2.50 paper; $3.75 cloth

The Journal of a Milledgeville Girl, 1861-1867
Edited by James C. Bonner
No. 4 $3.00

Confederate Imprints in the University of Georgia Libraries
Edited by Richard B. Harwell
No. 5 $2.00

The Mysterious Father: A Tragedy in Five Acts, 1807
By William Bulloch Maxwell
Edited by Gerald Kahan
No. 6 $2.50

Foreword to the Reissue

I met Lachlan McIntosh in 1972 during my second year of graduate study at the University of Georgia. I had been told by third-year students that if I wanted to finish as I planned, I needed to have a dissertation topic identified so that I could begin research during that second year and write a few seminar papers on the subject. This would allow me to get organized and focused. Taking this advice to heart, I approached Professor G. Melvin Herndon. He had agreed to direct my dissertation.

I told him that I would like to get started and asked if he had a topic in mind. The conversation, as I recall, went something like this:

Me: "Any idea on what I might write?"
He: "Ever heard of Lachlan McIntosh?"
Me: "No."
He: "Go check him out."

Thus began my relationship with the man who would be my close companion in the coming years—General Lachlan McIntosh.

Early on I discovered that the foundation for my work had already been laid by collectors, archivists, librarians, and editors—those important but often unsung heroes of historical scholarship who preserved, transcribed, and published McIntosh material that was scattered from as far north as Pennsylvania to as far south as Savannah. They made my task much easier.

Of these, the most gracious and helpful was Mrs. Lilla Mills Hawes, director of the Georgia Historical Society and editor of this collection. She was and remains the preeminent authority on the man we came to call "the General." Though this volume contains only the Lachlan McIntosh papers in the University of Georgia Libraries, its introduction and copious notes point the way to other McIntosh material, which, taken as a whole, reveal a treasure trove of eighteenth-century documents. They tell the story of how a colony became a state and how a man became a hero to many and a villain to others. So thorough was her research and so insightful was the introduction she wrote that there were times when I seriously wondered if there was much I could add.

Happily, for me, there was more to the McIntosh story. Happily, for you, what you have here are letters, reports, and accounts that take you into the heart of the colonial and Revolutionary eras in a depth seldom matched in similar collections. Though Lachlan McIntosh remains little known today outside of Georgia and a few locations in Western Pennsylvania and Ohio, his career placed him in the middle of critical events in the history of the nation he helped create and which he served well.

The incidents revealed in these papers tell the story of a country growing up and a man growing with it. From his arrival as a boy of eight, one of a contingent of Scots brought to Georgia to guard the colony's southern frontier from Spanish incursions, he and his family found themselves part of events larger than themselves. Outlined in Mrs. Hawes's introduction, these events serve as preliminaries to what is contained in the papers and give readers an idea of the frontier conditions that helped make the man.

The papers also illuminate the man himself. One such revelation is found in the oldest document in the collection, a 1755 wedding discharge, in which John and Ester Cuthbert not only give their daughter in marriage to Lachlan McIntosh but also promise "never to make any charge" to him for "her Board, Clothing, Lodging, Washing, Schooling, or any thing else whatsoever from her birth to this day." It was a document typical of a man wishing to enter into a relationship unencumbered by anything that might prevent him from doing what he intended when he intended.

Subsequent documents—some McIntosh collected, some he wrote—reveal a mature man with that same attention to detail, though in these later documents, the details were different. They mostly dealt with the growing strain between England's colonies, especially Georgia, and the Mother Country. Seldom are the American grievances better laid out than in the petition passed in 1775 by fellow members of the Darien Committee included here. Drafted and edited by McIntosh, it is one of the earliest statements of solidarity with the colonial cause to come from the lower South, and it marks an important turning point in the rise of the Whig movement in Georgia.

From that point forward the letters deal with items that range from the mundane (a request for a promised cask of rum, "as I am much in need of it") to the more significant, such as the management of labor (underscoring the degree to which the colony's economy depended on slaves). Contained here are accounts of the setting up of a Revolutionary government, the Council of Safety, and the organization of a military force under his command.

From the Revolution onward, documents that once dealt with plantation management turned to problems facing then-colonel Lachlan McIntosh and difficulties that a largely inexperienced commander faced in raising, training, and maintaining an army. True, he came from a Scottish military tradition, but how much of that prepared him for what lay ahead can only be surmised. Nevertheless, the widely held belief that the ability to lead was not something learned but was innate seems to have been proven in McIntosh. Despite his lack of formal training in strategy, logistics, and the art of war, at least on such a large scale, he displayed a talent for grasping a situation, placing resources where they were needed, and getting the best from his men. The promotion to general that soon followed was well deserved.

The letters also reveal a man sensitive to insult, especially when his reputation and that of his family were involved. When he acted in defense of his honor, he booked no quarter. A case in point was his well-known duel with Button Gwinnett, radical politician and signer of the Declaration of Independence. McIntosh passed this sensitivity along to his son, William, whose horsewhipping of George Walton, another signatory of the Declaration of Independence and the chief justice of Georgia, was little known until the publication of these papers. Walton had insulted William's father and family, something no gentleman could tolerate. In his defense, William denounced Walton, as his father had earlier denounced Gwinnett, and, declaring that such a scoundrel deserved whipping, confirmed that father and son were cut from the same cloth.

Hounded by his political enemies after Gwinnett's death, Lachlan McIntosh was transferred to Washington's army in Pennsylvania, where he endured the bitter winter of 1777–78 at Valley Forge. There he so impressed General Washington that in 1778 the future president put McIntosh in charge of the Western Department, and he served with distinction as commander of Fort Pitt. Significantly, he led an expedition that pushed American claims into the Ohio River Valley, where he established an outpost that he named for himself, Fort McIntosh. Modesty was not one of the general's virtues.

After returning to Georgia in 1779, he was part of the unsuccessful attempt to take Savannah from the British and an equally unsuccessful effort to defend Charleston from the same enemy. Included in the McIntosh papers and published here are journals of these trying times that were kept by McIntosh, John Habersham, and an unidentified subaltern. Taken prisoner when Charleston fell, McIntosh was subsequently exchanged and spent the rest of the conflict trying to provide for his wife and children, who were displaced by the fighting. The impact of the war was felt far beyond the battlefield.

When peace came, McIntosh returned to Georgia, where he hoped to resume life as he had known it. However, he found his plantations destroyed, his slaves stolen or strayed, and his financial future uncertain. No doubt inclined to sympathize, he maybe even agreed with his Loyalist friend and son-in-law, Robert Baillie, who, after the conflict, wrote that "this cursed War has ruirn'd us all." McIntosh spent considerable time and energy in efforts to gain compensation for his losses. These were only partially successful, so he left his Altamaha home and relocated to Savannah. There, still seeking the recognition he felt his due, he joined other officers of the Continental Army in forming the Order of the Cincinnati in 1783, a veterans' organization widely criticized by more-republican-minded Americans for harboring monarchist sympathies.

A man of decidedly conservative sentiments, McIntosh had political leanings similar to those of his much-admired commander George Washington and his close friend and financial partner Henry Laurens. He gave his support to the Philadelphia convention that drafted the new Constitution because of the men who wrote it, though he remained skeptical of the document itself.

Foreword

However, his other postwar problems were so great that he had little time for politics. Occasionally he was called on to serve the state in various capacities, appointments that recognized his ability to organize and negotiate but that also made the most of his reputation. The papers here make little mention of these. Instead, not surprisingly, the postwar documents he saved that have come down to us in this collection deal mostly with matters of business—who owed what to whom, how to prove losses when vouchers did not survive the war, how to get the new governments (state and national) to pay him what they owed, and how to get compensation from Britain for damages done and property taken during occupation.

Taken as a whole, it is a catalog of what McIntosh, and so many others like him, sacrificed for American independence.

During the last years of his life, McIntosh was a grand old man to many and an irritant to others. To himself and to his family and friends he remained true. When he died in Savannah on February 20, 1806, shortly before his seventy-ninth birthday, he had outlived most of the generation who had fought for American independence. He was buried in what is today Colonial Park Cemetery in Savannah with all the honors due a hero of the Revolution. He would have liked that.

HARVEY H. JACKSON III

Foreword

MR. Keith Read was a business man and book collector in Savannah. He sold most of his books before his death in 1940 but his collection of manuscripts survived him. For many years they were stored in a bank vault in Savannah, but in 1957 his heirs decided to sell them, and the Wormsloe Foundation of Savannah purchased and donated them to the University of Georgia Libraries.

The collection, consisting of 3,625 items, contains rare and unique pieces in the form of diaries, letterbooks, journals, and letters which reflect many facets of early Georgia history. Some items have already been published, one being the *Laws of the Creek Nation* which appeared as the first number in the *Miscellanea Publications*. The material for the present volume also is taken from the Keith Read Collection.

The papers of Major-General Lachlan McIntosh are of importance because they contain much information concerning the Revolutionary War in Georgia and of that period in our history. Part of his papers are owned by the Georgia Historical Society and were published as volume 12 of the *Collections* of the Georgia Historical Society in 1957. They were edited by Mrs. Lilla M. Hawes, Librarian of the Society. It was natural to turn to her for editing these additional papers of the same man. This volume should be considered as a companion volume to the earlier one.

W. P. Kellam, Director
University of Georgia Libraries

Introduction

IN 1735, two years after the first settlers arrived in Georgia, the threat of invasion by the Spanish in Florida demanded a military settlement south of Savannah. For this important post, which he had decided must be near the mouth of the Altamaha River, James Edward Oglethorpe commissioned Hugh Mackay and Captain George Dunbar to recruit a Highland company from Scotland.

So, on January 10, 1736, the *Prince of Wales*, Captain Dunbar, master, arrived in Georgia with 170 Scottish Highlanders—men, women, and children, most of them from near Inverness, and many of them descendants of survivors of the Jacobite uprising of 1715. William MacKenzie of Edinburgh, who was engaged in some investigation for the Georgia Historical Society, wrote in 1844 that "the government of the day were very happy to see the Ga. emigrants fairly out of Scotland as their connections all belonged to the Jacobite party." In another letter MacKenzie said, "I have ascertained, 1st. That those who emigrated to Ga. were men of good character, and that they were carefully selected for their military qualities. . . . Also, that those in authority among them, were highly connected in the Highlands."[1]

These Scots established their settlement on the Altamaha River near the ruins of Fort King George which had been abandoned in 1727. They named their town Darien in memory of the ill-fated late 17th century Scottish settlement on the Isthmus of Panama, which, after decimation by tropical diseases, the Spanish had forced them to abandon in 1700. Many of the same clans that came to Georgia had participated in the Darien Company as investors and/or settlers. Their naming this new settlement after the former one was an act of bravery and a defiance of the Spanish in Florida. In 1739 the district was called Darien, and the town was known for two or three years as New Inverness. Afterwards both town and district were known as Darien.[2]

John McIntosh Mor (Moor, Mohr[3]) of the Borlum branch, age 36, was the leader of the group. He was accompanied to Georgia by his wife, Margaret (or Marjorie) Fraser McIntosh, age 30; their sons, William, age 10; Lachlan (writer of the letters in this publication), age 9; John, age 8; Phineas, age 3; and the twins, Lewis and Janet, age about 14 months. Their daughter, Anne, and their son, George, were born in Darien in 1737 and 1739, respectively. The family Bible indicates that Phineas, Lewis, and Janet died young in Darien. The circumstances of the death in 1738 of Lewis was reported by William Stephens, "And at Darien, a most unhappy Accident befell Mr. McIntosh's Family, whose two Sons (young Lads) being swimming in the River, an Alligator snapped one, and carried him quite off."[4]

The Earl of Egmont referred to John McIntosh Mor as "Gent.; Chief of Darien." MacKenzie, mentioned above, wrote that "John M. McIntosh, previous to his going out with Oglethorpe, was a gentleman farmer—a class now extinct in the Highlands." In addition to his military duties he seems to have been an unofficial mentor and arbitrator of internal disputes. An early Savannah newspaper said of him, "Many of these new Emigrants, being all together, never learned the English language, and the whole lived in the greatest simplicity and harmony, having neither *Lawyers* nor Courts, but their differences all amicably settled by the decisions of their good old Captain."

At the unsuccessful siege of St. Augustine in 1740, John McIntosh Mor, Captain of the Highland Company, was captured at Fort Moosa by the Spanish and carried to Spain where he was held a prisoner for several years. Young William, who had followed his father to Fort Moosa, saw him fall, covered with blood from his wounds. He fled in panic just as he, too, was about to be captured. On being exchanged, John McIntosh Mor returned to Georgia, with his health broken from long confinement. He died in 1761 on his plantation, Essick, on Sapelo River. "He died prematurely, in the 63rd year of his age, by the quackery and ignorance of the *first Doctor* who ever tried to make his fortune amongst these honest patriarchs."[5]

William, the eldest son, was a cadet in Oglethorpe's Regiment and as such took part in the Battle of Bloody Marsh in 1742, though he was only sixteen at the time. He later became a planter on the Altamaha. In 1775 he was a delegate from St. Andrews Parish to the Provincial Congress in Savannah. In the early years of the Revolution he was a Colonel of Light Horse, but resigned his commission because of ill health. William remained in Georgia during the war as a prisoner on parole: his plantation was plundered by Tories and he suffered severe financial losses. He died in 1801.[6]

William's oldest son John is, next to Lachlan, the best known member of the family. John was a Lt. Colonel in the Revolution and issued the challenge, "Come and take it," to the British who demanded the surrender of Fort Morris. He was also a General in the War of 1812.

John, Jr., third son of John McIntosh Mor, left Georgia when he was about twenty-four years old. He died at his home, Hermitage, in St. Thomas' East in the Island of Jamaica in December 1786, at the age of sixty-nine. He left no family.[7]

Anne, the only surviving daughter, married Robert Baillie. The Baillies were Loyalists during the Revolution, but their political beliefs did not overrule their natural family affection, evidenced by the letter Robert Baillie wrote in 1781 to his brother-in-law, Lachlan, a Brigadier-General in the Continental Army and then in Philadelphia, having been recently exchanged as a prisoner of war, "I saw William & his family a few days ago. . . . This cursed War has ruin'd us all, however, I still flatter myself it will soon be at an End, and that we shall again be able to return to our Plantations & live peaceably together which I assure you I most sincerely wish for. . . . We are very anxious to hear where Mrs. McIntosh & the Children are. I hope you will now be able to have them with you, her present Situation in North Carolina must have been very disagreeable as it has been the Seat of War."[8]

George, the youngest child of John McIntosh Mor, when about eleven years old was taken to Charles Town by his brother Lachlan, and placed in a grammar school. "After he had acquired such other accomplishments as were then taught at that place," Lachlan wrote, he was "bound for four years to an Architect." Lachlan brought him back to

Georgia and had him appointed commissary of supplies for the troops at Frederica and other posts. He also instructed him in geometry and surveying, but his "inclination . . . led him to planting" and he soon became a large landholder in the parishes of St. John, St. Andrew, and St. Mary, also owning a lot in the town of Savannah. He married Ann Priscilla Houstoun, only daughter of Sir Patrick Houstoun. In 1764-1768 and 1772 he was a member of the Commons House of Assembly of Georgia, and in 1775 was a delegate to the Provincial Congress from St. Andrews Parish, as were his brothers, William and Lachlan. Early in the Revolution George was accused of furnishing rice and other supplies to the enemy in Florida. The Governor of Georgia ordered that he be sent to Philadelphia to stand trial by the Continental Congress, but Congress refused to try him because of insufficient evidence. Many historians believe that the charges against George were trumped up as a part of the plot to get rid of Lachlan as Continental Commander in Georgia. George died in 1779 and his considerable estate passed to his son, John Houstoun McIntosh, then about seven years old. His wife had died a few years before George.

Lachlan, whose papers in the Keith Read Collection in the University of Georgia Library are presented below, was the second son of John McIntosh Mor. Born in Badenoch in 1725, he came to Georgia as a child of nine years and readily fitted into life on the frontier. The forest wilderness bordering the Altamaha, contrasting strangely with his native Highlands, appealed to the youth. His brother William said of him, "there was not an Indian in all the tribes that could compete with him in the race." After his father's capture at Fort Moosa in 1740 and imprisonment in Spain, Lachlan and sister Anne were at Bethesda, the orphanage of the Rev. George Whitefield near Savannah, for their keep and education. While there Lachlan wrote dolefully of the orphanage, "The Spirit of the Lord I hope is beginning to blow among the dry Bones here. The House was never since I came thither liklier to answer the end of its Institution than now: Little Boys and little Girls, at this and that corner, crying unto the Lord, that he would have Mercy upon them." Lachlan left Bethesda on April 26, 1742, as he was "ordered by Gen.

INTRODUCTION 5

Oglethorpe to his regiment at Frederica being a cadet there." Anne also left Bethesda in 1742, and returned to her mother.[9]

Thomas Spalding, grandson of William McIntosh, wrote that as Oglethorpe was leaving Georgia, because of rumors of an invasion of England by the Young Pretender, the young McIntosh brothers, William and Lachlan, both members of Oglethorpe's regiment, were found hidden in the hold of another vessel. They, too, had heard the rumors and were anxious to return to Scotland to follow "Bonnie Prince Charlie." Oglethorpe ordered the two lads to his cabin, spoke to them at length, and persuaded them that the Stuart cause was hopeless and that their future lay in Georgia.[10]

In 1748 the twenty-one-year old Lachlan left Georgia and went to Charles Town where he worked for a number of years in the counting-house of Henry Laurens with whom he formed a warm and life-long friendship. On his return to Georgia he became a successful planter on the Altamaha River and a land surveyor. In January 1756 in Williamsburg, South Carolina, he married Sarah Threadcraft, daughter of George and Esther Lesesne Threadcraft.

In 1775 he was chairman of the committee of the lower district of St. Andrews Parish to elect delegates to the Provincial Congress in Savannah, and was himself elected one of the delegates.

His heritage as a member of a Highland-soldier family and his experience as a cadet in Oglethorpe's regiment contributed to his unusual ability in military affairs. In January 1776 he was appointed Colonel of the 1st Regiment, Georgia Line, and in September of that year he was promoted to Brigadier-General in the Continental Army. Button Gwinnett coveted the Continental command in Georgia and his jealousy and interference in military affairs created an animosity between the two men and a political intrigue which led to the well known duel on May 16, 1777. Both men were wounded; Gwinnett died within three days and McIntosh recovered. He stood trial, was acquitted, and was ordered to Headquarters for a new assignment. He was with Washington at Valley Forge in that terrible winter of 1777-1778, and afterwards was transferred to command of the Western Department, where he led an expedition against the Indians.

Two of the forts built at this time were given familiar names —Fort Laurens for his friend, Henry Laurens, then President of the Continental Congress, and Fort McIntosh for himself. Here, too, he was a subject of controversy.[11]

At his own request he was returned to Georgia in 1779 and led the Georgia Continental troops in the unsuccessful attempt to recapture Savannah with French assistance in September and October of that year. During the siege of the town his wife and five small children were stranded in Savannah, despite a formal request to General Prevost to permit them to leave. They were exposed to shot and shell from both sides; their belongings were plundered, and Mrs. McIntosh was reduced to "manual Labour."

In May 1780 McIntosh was captured at the fall of Charles Town and was for a time a prisoner of war. After being exchanged he continued in active service until the end of the Revolution, attaining the rank of Major-General. His family spent a semi-nomadic existence during these years, going from Savannah to South Carolina, to North Carolina, to Virginia, and back to Georgia at the end of the war. McIntosh wrote that "with only the bare Clothes they had on" they were "drove from place to place before the enemy . . . and obliged to exist on the bounty of such as might wish to assist."

Two of Lachlan's sons, Lachlan, Jr., and William, also served in the Revolution. Lachlan, Jr., attained the rank of Major and at different times was aide to his father and to Major-General Baron von Steuben and Inspector General of the Western Department. He died in Camden, South Carolina, in 1783 while escorting his mother and younger brothers and sisters back to Savannah after their long exile. William served during the entire war, beginning as Ensign in the 1st Regiment, Georgia Line, in 1776; he attained the rank of Captain in 1777 and was breveted Major in 1783.[12] Lachlan's oldest son, John, was in Jamaica with his Uncle John at the outbreak of the Revolution, and probably stayed there during the war, for no record of service for him has been found.

After the war Lachlan returned to Georgia and resumed planting. In 1783 he was one of the organizers of the Society of the Cincinnati, was elected the first president of the Georgia Society, and served in that capacity for several years. He was a delegate from Georgia to the Continental Congress in 1784, one of the commissioners for Georgia at the Hopewell treaty with the Cherokee Indians in 1785, and a commissioner for Georgia at the Beaufort Convention in 1787 which settled the boundary between Georgia and South Carolina. Except for the time he spent on his various plantations, his residence was in Savannah in the home he bought in 1777 after his Altamaha River plantation was plundered by Tories. He died in Savannah on February 20, 1806, shortly before his eightieth birthday.[13]

Though Lachlan was still a large landowner, the war had ruined him financially. At the time of his death he had not recovered from the state and nation the sums due him for his service or the money from his personal resources which he had put into the American cause. Nor had he and his friends entirely succeeded in vindicating him of the false charges deriving from the plot against him by the adherents of Gwinnett. Despite these charges he was respected and well liked. William Bartram, the naturalist, visited him in 1773 and wrote that he was welcomed by that "friendly man" who "smiling, & with a grace & dignity peculiar to himself, took me by the hand and accosted me thus: 'Friend Bartram, come under my roof, and I desire you to make my house your house, as long as convenient to yourself; remember from this moment, that you are part of my family'." The officers of the Georgia Continental Line declared "that they ever had, and do Still retain the highest respect for the General as a Gentleman, and approbation of his conduct as an officer, and that there is not another officer on the continent that they would prefer to the General to command them." Mordecai Sheftall referred to him as a man of "Strict probity and Honour."[14] That he was a devoted husband and parent, ardent advocate of the American cause, and an able military leader is evident in his papers.

No personal papers from the early years of Lachlan McIntosh's life have survived. Most of his papers were at one time in the collection of James Vallence Bevan who had been authorized by the State of Georgia in 1824 to write an official history of the state but whose untimely death in 1830 put an end to this project.[15] A few of the papers have been published before, as indicated in the footnotes. On the whole, they add little information to the known facts of McIntosh's life and career but supply considerable detail. They should be read in connection with "The Papers of Lachlan McIntosh, 1774-1799," published as *Collections of the Georgia Historical Society*, Vol. XII (Savannah, 1957), for the two collections, having once been a single collection, supplement each other. The account of the horse-whipping of George Walton, Signer of the Declaration of Independence and recently elected Chief Justice of Georgia, by William, Lachlan's son, was an unknown incident until it came to light in these papers. It seems a peculiarly fitting climax to the efforts of Walton to discredit General McIntosh.

Several of the papers in the collection could not be included in this publication because of the illegibility. Some of the papers included herein are badly mutilated. In many places they are torn and some parts are missing. I have added in brackets material to complete the meaning and have also inserted in brackets my interpretation of illegible words and phrases.

In editing the papers I have made few changes except occasionally in punctuation for clarification. Careless duplications of words have been omitted. No attempt was made to identify every person mentioned; most of them are so well known as to make this unnecessary.

I am indebted to Miss Bessie Lewis of Pine Harbor, McIntosh County, for her aid and advice.

Lilla Mills Hawes

Georgia Historical Society
Savannah, Georgia

PART I
Letters and Documents

"John & Esther Cuthbert discharge to their Daughter Sarah Threadcraft before her Marriage 31 December 1755. No. 2"[1]

We Promise both & either of us for ourselves our Heirs &ca. never to make any Charge, or come upon Lachlan Mackintosh his Heirs Exors or Admors upon the Account of our Daughter Sarah Threadcraft for her Board, Clothing, Lodging, Washing, Schooling or any thing else whatsoever from her birth to this day as Witness our Hands in Williamsburgh So. Carolina this 31st. day of Decemr. 1755.

[Signed] John Cuthbert
Esther Cuthbert[2]

After the above promise was obtained Lachlan Mackintosh and Sarah Threadcraft were Married the next day, first day of January 1756.

"Extract of Letter Mercurious" [1774][3]

Extract from a Letter &ca from a Gentn. in Carolina

What good will not some People oppose, or what absurditys & Errors wickedness & injustice have not found Advocates, even to the very Denying of our Senses & justifying the most horrid Crueltys & persecutions of our own Species. this has not only been done by Laymen but also by those whose Sacred function bound them to inculcate the Law of peace meekness Charity & truth by their Doctrin & Example such is the Weakness of Humanity when under the influence of a sordid Intent & depending on a Corrupt Court. I was insensibly Led into these reflections on pursuing as far as my Patience would allow some pieces lately published in your Georgia Gazette attempting to Justifie some late Acts of the Brittish Legislature & tho' under different Signatures appear to be the work of the same worthy persons seemingly the joint Effort of a warmplace Man a Sophistical Dabler in Law & a vain pedagogue, the latter of whom will probably be rewarded with permission to father the glorious production.

Were the Brittish parliament to impose the Laws & Religion of Turkey on all America as they have done that of Paris in great part of it those wretched Advocates would find pretexts to Justifie it. perhaps our kind parent not caring to trust the Government of her children in their own Hands as they are not come to the perfect use of their Senses or feeling yet, would find it Necessary for a Season kindly to learn them entire Submission & obedience, or it might be called a Mild Chastisement for some Undu[ti]full Conduct or Crime trumpt up against us to bring us to reason. Ye Gods! can you Suffer your best your Noble & disting[uish]ing Gift reason to be thus perverted by Man!

- - - - - - - - - -

In the Darien Committee Thursday 12th. January 1775.[4]

When the most Valuable Privileges of a People are Invaded not only by op[en] Violence, but by every kind of Fraud Sophistry & Cunning, it behooves every Individual [to] be upon his Guard, and every part of the Society like Beacons in a Country Sur[round]ed by Enemies to give the Alarm, not only when their Libertys in General are attacked but Separately, least a precedent in one may affect the whole, and to enable the Collective Wisdom of such People to Judge of its Consequence, and how far their respective Grievances concerns all, or shou'd be opposed to preserve their necessary & willin[g Union?] Every Laudable attempt of this kind by the good People of this Colony in a Constitutionall manner hath been hitherto frustrated by the Influence & Authority of Men in Office & their Numerous Dependants, and in every other Natural & Just way by the Various Arts they have put in practice. We therefore, the Representatives of the Extensive District of Darien in the Colony of Georgia, being now Assembled in Congress by the Authority and free Choice of the Inhabitants of the said District now freed from their fetters do RESOLVE

1st. That the unparaleled Moderation the decent but firm & Manly Conduct of the Loyal and Brave People of

Boston & Massachuetts Bay to preserve their Liberty deserves not only the applaus & thanks of all America, But also the admiration (*Imitation*)* of all [the] world (*Mankind*), But to avoid needless repetitions we acquiece & Join in all the Resolutions passed by the Grand American Congress in Philadelphia last October, we thank them for their Sage Counsel & advice, and most Heartily & Chearfully Accede to the Association entered into by them as the Wisest & most Moderate Measure that could be adopted in our present Circumstances to Reconcile & firmly Unite Great Brittain & the Colonys so indispensably necessary to each other, by the Surest & best Basi[s,] Mutual Interest. But as the Wisest Councils upon Earth are Lyable to the [Errours] of Humanity, & notwithstanding our Reverence & partiality for that August As[sembly] we begg Leave to differ in opinion from them, in charging the unjust Mea[sures] of the Present & preceeding Ministry to a person quallifyed rather for a Private than a Public Station, & as the Resentment of his Country Men on a former occas[ion] was raised by the illiberal & unjust abuse of them indiscriminately for the Fau[lts] of that Man, we humbly Presume the Renewing (*Remembrance*) it at this Time on so little foundation *at Least Impolitick* being confident that every Member of that late wise Patriotick, & truly Honourable Congress from a Principle of Can[dour] & Justice will rather commend than blame our honest & well Meant freedom.

2d. That the Shutting up the Land Offices the Scheme (*intention*) of raising our quit Rents, & Setting up our Lands to (*at*) Publick Sale, Degrading the Representatives of our Sovereign (*the Crown to Action*) into Paltry Auctioneers—quere if any quit Rents are Just or Legal—have not been duly considered (& attended to) in all its consequences to this Vast Continent. that [it] is a principle part of the unjust System of Politicks adopted by the present Ministry to sub-

---

*McIntosh, in drafting a paper often wrote a word or phrase above another word or phrase within a brace, showing a choice of expression for the final draft. These papers have been transcribed with the second word and phrase in parentheses following the original. To distinguish between McIntosh's own parenthetical material and the added words or phrases, the latter are set in italics.

ject & Enslave us, & evidently proceeds from an ungene[rous] Jelousy of the Colonys to prevent as much as possible the population of America & the Relief of the poor and Distressed in Brittain & elsewhere for whom a kind Providence has opened (*disclosed*) a New World from their Merciless Oppressor when the old is overrun with them (*such Monsters*). That Monopolising (& shou'd be free to all) our Lands into few Hands is forming & encouraging Petty Tyrrants to Lord it over us, or Reside in any other part of the World in Extravagance Luxury & Folly by the fruit of our Labour & Industry. Such oppressions neither we nor our Fathers were not able to bear & drove us to this Wilderness and that all encouragement shou'd be given to the poor of every Nation by every generous American.

[3d.] That M[inisteri]al Mandates commonly called (*under the name of*) Instructions preventing the Legal Representatives of the People to make (*Enact–Frame*) Laws Suiting their own Respective Situations & Circumstances are a general Grievance, Repugnant to the priviledges of free Brittish Subjects & the Natural Rights of all Mankind* & more especially in this Youn[g] Colony where our Internal Pollice [Policy] is not yet well Settled (*Fixed*), & as a Proof of (*or, to demonstrate*) the Intention of these restrictions when Time & opportunity offers, we point out (*Instance*) particularly amongst many others of the Like Nature the not Suffering us to Limit the Term (*Continuance*) of our Assemblys, or passing a Quit Rent Law to ascertain & fix the most valuable part of our Property.

4thly. That an over proportion of Officers for the Number of Inhabitants, and paying their Salerys from Brittain, so much cast up to us by Court Parasites, & for which we are so often charged (*told*) with Ingratitude, are in truth real & great Grievances rendering them Insolent & regardless of their Conduct, being Independent of the People who shou'd Support them according to their Usefullness & behaviour, and also for whose Benefit (*advantage*) & conveniency alone they were originaly intended, that besides these exhorbitant Salerys

---

*McIntosh sometimes lined through phrases on his manuscript. These deletions are shown as McIntosh marked them.

which enables them all to Act by Deputies whilst they wallow in Luxury themselves, their Combining to rais[e] their Exhorbitant illegal Fees & Perquisites by various arts upon the Subject to an alarming hight, as if formed with Long Claws like Eagles are more dangerous to our Liberties than a Regular Army having the Means of Corruption so much in their power, the danger of which is iminently Exemplifyed in the Present unhappy State of our Bretheren & fellow Subjects in Brittain and even in the Late Conduct of this Colony. To remedy (*prevent*) therefore as much as in us Lyes these direfull Effects, *We do Resolve* never to Choose any Officer (*Person in public Office*) his Deputy, Deputies Deputy their Tools or any Expectant to Represent us in Assembly or any other Publick place in our Election--hoping the Example will be followed throughout this Colony & all America.

[5th.] To shew the World that we are not influenced by any Contracted or Intended Views (*motives*), but a general Philanthropy for all Mankind of whatever Climate Language or Complection, We hereby declare our disaprobation and abhorrence of the Unnatural Practice of Slavery in America, (however the Uncultivated State of our Country or other Specious arguments may be plead for it) A Practice founded in Injustice and Cruelty, and highly dangerous to our Libertys (as well as Lives) debasing part of our own Species (*fellow Creatures*) below Men, & Corrupting the Virtue & Morals of the rest, & is Laying the Basis of that Liberty we Contend for (& which we pray the Almighty to preserve for Ages (*Continue to the latest posterity*) upon a quite (*very*) wrong Foundation. We therefore Resolve at all Times to use our Utmost endeavours for the Manumission of our Slaves in this Colony upon the most Safe and equitable footing for the Masters and themselves.

[6th.] That we do hereby Choose Messrs. [blank] to Represent us [for this] District in the Provincial Congress at Savannah the 18th. Instant or at any other Time & place appointed hereafter for the Space of one year (*Six months*) from this Day and that a Copy of these our Resolutions be given them as expressing the Sense of this District of public Grievances, which will Serve for their direction and Instructions, and it is further our desire that our said Deputys shall Use their Endeavours to Send two Delegates from this Colony to the general Continental Congress to be held at Philadelphia next May.

- - - - - - - - - -

McIntosh to George Houstoun.

Darien 26th [?] July 1775

Dear Sir,

Inclosed I send you a Letter I received Yesterday from John Simpson & Co. of Charlestown acquainting me that my two Negro Fellows Ben & Glascow are in the Work House there, and I shall depend upon you to get these Gentn. Jacob Valk, or any other Person in Charlesto. who you think will do me Justice to Sell them to the best advantage & *as soon* as possible to save any further Expence or risque. I mentioned to you on a former occasion that I was determined to dispose of them, as they got acquainted with that Villain the Indian Doctor who conveyed them to the Nation & Lives in our Neighborhood altho they are the most Valuable Slaves I own, being both good Sawyers Squarers Boatmen & Shingle makers as well as Field Slaves, & no runaways untill they were decoyed away this Time which can be no disadvantage where they are at [a] Distance from the Indian Doctor, as neither of them are Woodsmen. Ben is also my Cooper, he is a Stout strong well made Fellow about 40 years of age & speaks a Little French which he Learned as well as English in his own Country Glascow a Slim neat made Fellow about 25 Year old & I think something taller than Ben, both of the Corrsmann or Congo Country. You know best how to Serve me in this matter to the best advantage, & begg you will not Neglect it & you will oblige Dr. Sir

Yr. most obt. Servt.
[Signed] Lachn. McIntosh

Pray send my Cask of Rum as soon as Possible as I am much in need of it. I hear it is very Cheap now. please to forward the inclosed by the Post.

Endorsed: Mr. George Houstoun[5]
Mercht. in Savannah

"Act of Council of Safety at Savannah 1 March 1776. relative to Shipping & exportation Recd. 4 March—"[6]
In the Council of Safety, Savannah, March 1st. 1776.

Whereas the Resolution of the honorable the Continental Congress, restraining the exportation of Rice from the united Colonies for a time, having expired this day, without any further, or additional Restraint, as we know of; it now lies with the Council of Safety for this Province, either further to restrain the exportation, or to permit it: And whereas a formidable force, both by Sea and Land, having invaded this Province for several Weeks past, & it appearing, by the arrival of such force, that the Cause of the said Continental Restriction is not yet removed:

Resolved, therefore, that no Ships loaded with Rice, or any other Article of Produce, in this Province shall be permitted to sail, without leave of the Council of Safety, or next Congress, except such Vessels, as are or shall be permitted to sail for the purpose of procuring the necessary means of defence.

Resolved, that, in case any loss shall be sustained by such detention, the Delegates for this Province shall be instructed to apply to the Continental Congress to make the reimbursement for such loss a general Charge.

Ordered, that the Rudders be unshipped & the Rigging & Sails taken away & secured, from the several Vessels now riding in the port of Savannah.

    Orders to Colonel Lachlan McIntosh.
Sir,
You will enforce & have executed the aforementioned Resolutions & Order; the Resolution heretofore delivered to you, as of the Council of Safety, being erroneous, and any permit you may have given in consequence, you will please to recall.
    By Order of the Council of Safety
     Wm. Ewen, Prest.
A true Copy from the Minutes
 Edwd Langworthy, Secy.

"To General [Charles Lee] 26th Augt. 1776."[7]

May it please your Excellency

Sir

I beg Leave in the name of the officers of the Georgia Battalion to offer some reasons for excepting the pre[cedency] of the South Carolina Regiments. Our's and three Battalions for that [Colony upon] Continental Establishment, [were ordered on one and the same day by the General Congress. Thus far we were upon a footing, unless being farther removed from the seat of Government and consequently more exposed to the] Enemy we might not be thought [worthy of] the post of Honor; for we apprehend the late Resolve of the General Congress, setting the rank of the South Carolina Regiments the 4th November last, tho' very favorable (all things considered) to them, does not exclude our having rank the same day. We desire not, Sir, to depreciate, or take from, the merit of our Brethren of South Carolina—they have gloriously repulsed a formidable British Fleet and Army, to their immortal Renown. We humbly presume we shewed the laudable Example, to that wealthy Colony in repelling [a force] equally formidable, in comparison of our weak and defenceless Situation, with these essential differences in our Circumstances, that most of our fellow Citizens and by far the most weighty, were either Neutral or joined our Enemy that a single R[egiment did not come to] the assistance of 4 or 500 dis[orderly and Raw Militia in the day of our distress. And more than *all* that we had] not the Military [reputation of a General Lee to] *inspire* us or *intimidate* [our] Enemies. [But decency requires, Sir] that we [say little on this head as] the generous and the brave, we are sure, will ever do us ample Justice, when they know the difficulties we surmounted. If we compare the Merits of the two Provinces, in another point of View, we flatter ourselves it will not prove less favorable to us. The Resolve of the Supreme and Venerable Senate was no [sooner known] than we instantly and implicitely obeyed, and acquiesced in every tittle of it whilst our Sister Colony (without entering into her motives) only apply'd for rank, and the pay allow'd her three Battalions, in aid of her own Expences; raised two new Regiments, and con[tinued] their old upon the Continental Establishment, and altogether under [their own direction and] provincial Commissions [which we dare venture to assert your Excellency must have often found] detrimental to the [general cause] and the Service at large—the Commissions so much insisted upon, by these Gentlemen, were sent to us, blank, and might have been dated the 4th. November, which doubtless was intended by the General Congress as the Pay was so small, to enable the Officers to furnish themselves with Arms, Uniforms &ca. but from a principle of generosity which would not permit them to receive any Pay untill they entered upon ser[vice] they were dated so late as the 29th. of January last; which we humbly conceive should rather be rewarded with Honor than otherwise. I am so little tenacious of my own Rank, that I will cheerfully give it up to men of such Merits as the Colonels Gadsden and [Moultrie] upon condition my Regiment has [the precedence] I think so justly due to it.

[I hope] Your Excellency will [take these]reasons into further consideration and [have the]
    Honor to be Your Excellency's
    Most obedient and most humble Servant
  [Signed] Lachn. McIntosh, Colo.
Savannah in Georgia
26 August 1776

Georgia   House of Assembly 28 Augt. 1777[8]
 On the Petition of Lachlan McIntosh & John Wereat Esqrs.
 Ordered That it be taken into Consideration next Tuesday Morning & that they be heard by their Council, & that there be a Call of the House on that Day.
    Abstract from the Minutes
    [Signed] H. Cuyler, C[lerk]

  "Colo. Baker 29th. Augt. 1777"[9]
    Midway August 29th. 1777
Sir-
 Yours per Capt. Salter I have received and observe the Contents. You inform me you have many Complaints with respect to the Regiment of Horse, and it would become neglect of your duty to Over look them.

Sir, I would by no means have you to over look a[ny] complaints respecting the Regiment of Horse or Offi[cers] comanding the same. If I have acted or done any [thing] to the Disadvantage of the State I am always ready [to] answer for the same.

It is true your orderd me to the Westward for the Troops, I accordingly proceeded up and gave orders to the officers of each respective Troop, to meet me in a reasonable time at Augusta in order to March from thence, with me to the Southward, but behol[d] instead of their marching their men agreable to [orders] they came themselves and told me, their men would [not] come unless they were immediately paid, now these [officers are not ?] fit to hold Commissions, yet seems to be Countinan[ced].

On my way from the Westward, I call'd and acquainted [you] with these particulars yet I seems to be reflected on f[or] coming down without a man. no person of any reason could have expected that I would have attended a parcell of footmen from Augusta. (as I had inform'd you the most of them had lost their horses.) and the weather so prodigious hot and my Self very unwell at the time.

I thought I had done my duty when I had given my Orders to the officers of each Troop, and if they had a mind to come down themselves, they Certainly if they had any Spirit would have oblig'd their men to obey Orders, but if officers are unwilling to obey orders, we need not wonder at the mens Disobeying orders.

I am afraid we have not got many officers that has the Good of the State at heart.

The reason of my not acquainting you of the Slaughter near fort Howe was I heard that Coll. Screven, Major McIntosh & Major Baker was up there after the Skirmish, and made no doubt, but one or the o[ther] of them had acquainted you with the particulars, indeed at that time it was out of my power to acquaint you being sick aBed.

If you recollect I mention'd to you some time agoe that Doctr. Callender neglected the Sick and that I should be under the necessity of looking out for another Surgeon. I have repeatedly spoke to the Doctr. but all to no purpose.

I have also spoke to the paymaster & his Excuse is that

he attends in Savannah till he is tir'd out and can but seldom get more than half money Enough to pay off the Troops.

As for the officers, being detained in Savannah for the want of their Accounts being properly Certify'd must be their own seeking, they must know that I do not reside in Town, and I never refus'd Certifying any Accounts that I thought was Just and I had a right to Certify. In Short I find there is no given Satisfaction. therefore Sir, I do now acquain[t] you that in future if you should send orders not to direct them to me as Coll. of the Regiment of [Horse] as I am Determin'd not to act in that Capaci[ty] any longer.
    I am Sir
     Your most obt. & very Hble [Servt.]
   [Signed] John Baker

P.S. there is at my fort 20 men arrived from the Westward & three of them deserted last night. I have sent after them— is all that is come down as [yet]

Endorsed:
 To the Honble Brigadier General McIntosh
 Savannah
favour'd Capt. Salter

[The following list of officers in McIntosh's hand is on the back of Col. Baker's letter:]

Capt. Habersham	Lieut. Milton
Henley	Roche
L McIntosh	Scrimger
Wright	W. McIntosh
Berrien	J. Bryan
Delaplaign	Glascock
G Walton	Neatherland
Cuthbert	Surzedas [sic]
	L. McIntosh
	J. Walton
	Ens. Brown

- - - - - - - - - -

 The United States of America To Lachn. McIntosh Dr[10]
1777
Octob. 10th   To Cash paid for Horses &ca. to carry
      himself & servant from Georgia to   Dols

Decr. 17th   Camp in Complyance with an order
                of Congress   800

                To Expences upon the Road from
                Savannah in Georgia to Head Quar-
                ters in Camp, where he arrived this
                Day   620
                                               Dols.   1420
Copy of Accot. the 16th May 1777
            - - - - - - - - - -

"Killed & wounded & prisoners of the British—Since the Commencemt. of the Warr to the latter end of 1777."[11]

In March 1776 the Parliment of Great Brittain granted Supplies for the Support of 42,390 Brittish and forreign Troops to serve in America Exclusive of 8000 Marines for that Campaign, which Military Stores was Shipped for and actually did land on the Continent before the 1st. Septr. following amounting to 50,390 land and Sea Forces, which was reduced by the Armys of the United States as follows. Vizt.

Commencement of Hostilitys	Killed	Wounded	Prisrs.
At Lexington and Concord	43	70	
At the Battle of Bunkers Hill	746	1105	
Ticonderoga, St. Johns and before Quebeck	81	110	340
On the Lakes by Genl. Arnold	53	64	
At the attack on Fort Moutry So. Carolina	197	260	
At the Ceadars in Canada	40	70	
At Norfolk & Great Bridge	129	115	40
At Different Engagements on long Island	840	1600	65
At Harlem & hell Gate Bridge	136	157	49
At New York Landings	57	100	
White Plains	350	490	200
At the attack at Fort Washington	900	1500	
Fort Qu[ebec]	20	35	
At Trenton 26th. Decr.	35	60	948
Prince Town	74	100	
Boston by Commodore Hardings	52	90	750
in Sundry Transports			390

LETTERS AND DOCUMENTS

At Danbury	260	350	
Iron Hill, New Castle County	59	80	20
At Brandy Wine 11th. Septr.	800	1170	
On reading Road by Genl. Maxwell	40	60	
On Statton Island by Genl. Sullivan	94	150	278
At Bennington 4th. Octr.	900	1300	30
Fort Miflin & Read banks	328		84
At Forts Montgamry & Clinton	580	700	
Of the Army undr. Genl. Borgoyne	2100	1126	5752
Prisonrs Surrendred and Diserters			1100
British & forriegn Troops Killed wounded & taken Prisoners Since the Commencement of Hostilitys in America	8894	11023	10046

29960 Total [sic]

Lachlan McIntosh, Jr. to Colonel [Joseph Habersham][13]
Dear Colonel,
My Duty requires that I shoud give you some accot. of my Journey & proceedings. I Accompanyed my Father through So. & No. Carolina & part of Virginia, where he left me to be Inoculated for the Small pox. & came up with him again in Camp at the Valley Forge Pensylvania the 13th Feby. after I recovered where I now am. I have Since traveled almost through the whole State of Jersey & great part of this for the sole purpose of Recruiting, without Engaging a Single man nor [did] I get any one of Reputation to accept of the Commission you was pleased to give me, & in short you may assure yourself the Recruiting Service in the old way is over which Congress are Sensible of, & will advance no more Mo[ney] & you need not send any more Officers upon that business here after for this there are many reasons. the Jealousy & Interested Policy of No. Carolina & Virginia produced a Law prohibiting any other State from Recruiting in either of theirs. my Father applyed to the Assembly of No. Caro. for a Repeal of the Law, or at least a Clause in favour of Georgia, & particularly the first Regiment without Effect. which discouraged him from attempting it in Virginia. the Substitute Law again recommended by Congress & adop-

[Retur]n of Military Stores at Fort Pitt March 1st 1778[12]

Item	Row 1	Row 2	Row 3	Row 4	Row 5
Muskets	(Mutilated)				
Cannon	8		8		8
Cannon Carriages	8		8		8
Cannon Cartridges	100		100		100
Empty Cannisters	300		300		300
Spunges & Rammers	13		13		13
Ladles & Worms	6		6		6
Bricoles & Ropes	2		2		2
Pieces (?) of Quick Match	200		200		200
Staves & Sadles	6		6		6
Lint & Port Fire Stocks	17		17		17
Priming Wires	2		2		2
Empty Paper Cartridges for Cannon	242		242		242
Boxes of Musket Cartridges	2		2		
Cartouche Boxes	266	20	286	110	176
Pouches & Horns	42	2	44	44	— 132
Bayonet Slings	161	6	167	35	
Bayonets	24	9	33	32	1
Camp Kettles	14	1	15	4	11
Tampons	775	14	789	276	513
Knapsacks	964	3	967	238	629
Canteens	680	14	694	[?]	[?]
Flints	6704		6704	993	5711
Brimstones & Wires	291		291		291
4 Lb Balls	203		203		203
5 Lb Balls	2125		2125	2125	
12 Lb B[alls]	1422		1422	1422	
[Illegible]	197		197	197	
[Illegible]	19.		[?]	[?]	

Erro[rs] Excepted

ted by all the States, was a great error, as many Men Offer 4 or 500 Dollars for a Man to excuse them from Military Duty. this State gives (*offers*) 100. Dollars besides the Continental bounty to every Man who will Inlist for three Years or during the Warr, & the New England States twice (*double*) that Sum to no purpose; & now they are all Resolved to fill their Several quotas of Troops by Draughts from their Militia. they have accomplished it already in New England, and they are *now* (*at this time*) marching to Camp. they are following their Example in Virginia & it is expected they will in all the other States by which it is to be hoped we shall have a fine Army by the time the Campaign opens. by this Sir, you must see how Needless my attempt was, however diligent I might be, & how disagreeable my disapointment is as well as my Situation otherwise, without Money, either for Recruits, if they could be had, or the Enormous Expences of Travelling at this time & without a Friend of our 1st. Regimt. in Congress to asist me. but as I can do nothing else to Serve my Country & the Corps I belong to, I will take the Liberty Genl. Howe & yourself were kind inough to give me of Staying some time in Camp to gain [some] knowledge & Experience in the Profession I have chose, wherein I flatter myself I will be indulged especially as you have Officers enough for the Men we have & hope you will Signify your approbation by applying to Genl. Howe & honoring me with a few Lines as soon as possible. & I can assure you Sir that I woud require some time to Save, as a twelve Months pay will not carry me back to Georgia in the frugalist manner.

The Season afords nothing New to inform you except little Skirmishing between foraging partys of no Consequence. Howe & his Army keep close in Philadelphia, the [illegible] Brittish parliament I suppose you have heard have voted 2,000 more Troops to his Asistance but where they are to be had, the Lord knows, unless it is the Russians[14] whom they have so Long tryed to Scare us with, though that Number if they could get them will hardly make up for their losses last Campaign. there are Some on both Sides appointed to meet at German town & Settle an Exchange of prisoners which tho Humanity Gratitude & Justice requires it of us, I think will be to our disadvantage at this time as it will be giving our Enemys so many Men, while the time of ours are all Expired & they will return home.

My Father tells me he wrote you by Capt. Jo. Lane abot. two Months ago & Says he will not write to you again until he receives a Letter from you, he joins me in Compliments to you Mrs. H and your Brothers. I begg you will deliver the Inclosed to my Mother & am Dr. Colonel

Yr. most obt. Hble Servt.

[Unsigned]

Camp Valley Forge Pensylvania
March 1778

April the 2 1778 general Mcintosh Dr.[15]

to 2 gallins of Bear	lb	1 - 0 - 0
to Dito 2 gallins of Bear		1 - 0 - 0
to Dito 2 gallins of Bear		1 - 0 - 0
to Dito 2 gallins of Bear		1 - 0 - 0
to Dito 1 gallin of Bear		0 - 10 - 0
to Dito 2 gallins of Bear		1 - 0 - 0
to 2 Quarts of Whisky		0 - 12 - 0
Sum total	lb	6 - 2 - 0

[Figures in McIntosh's hand on verso]:

```
 6
 6
 2
 2
―――
16-24/90 Dollars
```

"Accot. my Expences Travelling round Hospitals 1778"
Left Camp Saturday Evening

		Dols.
4th. April -	pd. Folk forage	1
5th.	pd. for Cyder & feed	2
	pd. at Webbs Cyder	1-1/3
	pd. Dinner & fee over Carwells Ferry	3-2/3
	pd. at Oakum's Lodging & Horses	3-1/2
6th.	pd. at penny town for Breakfast &ca.	4
		Dols. 15-1/2

LETTERS AND DOCUMENTS 25

9th.   pd. at Bergen's for
             Horses Sevrt. &ca.   9-1/2
10th.   pd. at William's Trenton   17-1/6
         pd. [blank] Tavern   1-2/3
         pd. at Flemington   2-1/6 [?]
[Parenthetical note: Barber from 20 Dec. to 20 Apr. 4 Mos.]
             Memmorandums 15th. May 1778[16]
Barbers Accot.—Washer Wms. accot.
ditto. Colo. Patton. Capt. B. Williams
Berrien qd.:—Cheesborough for Ration.—Dr. Bond. 106
Colo. Gibson 80—Laurens 1500.
Settle Expences from Georgia for Thomson, Lack & Self—
Get Horses, Waggon, Tent.—Shoes, Blankets, Linnen &ca.
pay & Rations for Lack & Self. Settle Correspondence.
Capt. Rices Accot. for Clot[hes ?]
Major Murphree for snuff [?]
Sutlers—Fitter Taylor
My Expences to Fort pit.—
Genl. Orders from Varin [?]
Mr. Boyd 31 Dollars—
Barber 8. Dollars. Sutler £621.
Lottery Tickets York.—Blankets
Blyth £3.—

- - - - - - - - - - -

[The following notes in McIntosh's hand are on this manuscript]:
    Acct. of Rations 17th. Decr. a 17 May 1778.
    Mr. Cheesburrough
    Mr. Berrien   4
    Thos. Gilmore   1
    Nicholas Blank   1
    David Edwards   1
    Jordan Rozier   1
    Wm. Low Fisher   1
    Genl. McIntosh   12
        Rations   21 per Day
        5 Mos. is   150
                                ————
                                1050
                                  21
                                ————
                                3150

Account of Provisions Issu'd to Genl. McIntosh's Mess Camp Valley Forge May 17, 1778[17]

Dates	By whom Order'd	Flour lb	Bread lb	F. Beef lb	S. Beef lb	S. Pork lb	F. Pork lb	Mutton lb	Salt Gills	Soap lb	Candles lb	Rice Gills	Spirits Gills	Salt Tongues No.	Herrings lb	Salt Fish lb
Jany.																
2	John Berrien M.B.		15													
7	ditto		10													
9	ditto		15													
12	ditto		20	23					4							
	do.			135					8		2		96			
18	do.			165					8		3					
20	do.		30													
25	do.		20													
26	do.															
27	do.		110	323					20		5		96			
Feby.																
1st.	do.		30			20			8	6		28	192	2	10	
2	do.		30	130											10	
5	do.		30	20		15			15		1½		96			
7	do.		30		12				16				64	4		
8	do.		20		12								64	6	12	
12	do.		10													
	do.		150	150		35			39	6	1½	28	224	12	32	

Acct. of Provisions Issu'd to Gen. McIntosh's Mess (Continued)

Date													
March 3	to Gilmore	30	165				8	6		92	00		
		7½	6				8						
11			22		12								
14		30											
16	Major Berrien			7									
17	do.		165	7									
20	do.	50			21½		16	6					
21	to Gilmore	10	7										
25	do.	10		10									
29	do.	30		10	19	12	32	12	6	92	224	12	32
	Amount carried Over	167½	365	22	54	12	91	6	18½	120	224	12	32
		427½	838										
1778	Brot Over	427½	838	22	54	12	91	6	18½	120	224	12	25
Apl. 1st	to Gilmore	30	12	23								12	
3	do.	30			15½							9	
5	do.	30	20					8	6		48	12	
7	do.												
8	do.		15										
9	do.	30	6										
10	do.	30											
13	do.		25										
11	do.		20										
16	do.	30	15	15								3	
18	do.	30	19				8		1				
21	do.	30	86				8		6				
23	do.											3	
24	do.	30	50					6					
27	do.												
29	do.	30					24	14	13		48	6	20
30	do.	300	253	15	15	15½							53 25

Acct. of Provisions Issu'd to Gen. McIntosh's Mess (Continued)

Dates	By whom order'd	Flour lb	Bread lb	F Beef lb	S Beef lb	S Pork lb	F Pork lb	Mutton lb	Salt Gills	Soap lb	Candles lb	Rice Gills	Spirits Gills	Salt Tongues No.	Herrings (?) lb	Fish lb
May 1	Major Berrien			28												
2	Capt. DuVal			54												
3	do.		30	50												
7	Major Berrien	30		50												
1	do.															
?	Capt. DuVal								8		6		88			
15	Do.															
?	Genl. McIntosh			28									2½			
?	Do.															
?	Capt. DuVal								8							
	Total	30	30	210		30			16		6		2¾			
		30	757	1301	45	99	12	36¾	131	20	37½	145	365¼	18	85	25

This is to Certify that the above Acct. is a true Copy from my Book
The different Species of Provision in this Accot. equal to 1172 full Rations

[Signed] John Cheesborough A.C. of Issue

LETTERS AND DOCUMENTS 29

"Colo. Brodhead 24 June '78—with answer"[18]
Lancaster June 24th. 1778.
Dear General,
I have been at great pains to get my Regt. properly equipped for the Western Expedition, but as almost every part of the Cloathing in the Cloathier General's Possession was assined before my arrival, I am under the disagreeable necessity of waiting several Days longer for cloathing.

The Armourers also notwithstanding the greatest exertions of my officers go on slowly in repairing the Arms.

I was very desirous to have the Rifles with Bayonets, which I had seen at Mr. Henry's Store; but they are sent to Northumberland & Bedford Counties, to arm the Fractious Inhabitants.

The Quarter Master [General and his] assistants, have been very oblidging & have exerted themselves to have me equipped, & I have drawn from them several necessary Articles, which I feared had escaped your attention.

I am exceeding anxious to be with you, & am much distressed for the unhappy fate of my fellow Citizens, on the frontiers; but should I March without being equipped with Cloathing, & proper Arms, I could not promise myself to do that Service, which otherwise might be expected from me.

Please to inform me whether it be your pleasure, that our Men should have Carriages to transport their Packs, as that would greatly facilitate the March.

Only fifty Blankets can be furnisht my Regt., & these arrived yesterday. I have employed the Taylors & Woolman [?] of my Regt., in making over all the shi[rts ?], of which not more than half the number wanted are Compleat.

I this Moment was favoured with yours of this date, and will immediately see your orders strictly complied with.

You may depend on my Marching for York, the Moment my Regt. is supplied with the necessary Cloathing.

I have the honour to be Dr. General
Your most obedt. Servt.
[Signed] Daniel Brodhead

Honble. Genl. McIntosh
Endorsed: (On Public Service)
    Honble. Brigadier Genl. McIntosh
    York
    Per Express
Daniel Brodhead of the P[ennsylvania] R[egiment]
[McIntosh's reply, written on the same letter.]
                            25th. June 1778. York[19]
Sir—
    I received yours of yesterday. I have to inform you that our expedition required we should be all ready, to sett of[f] from Fort Pitt, the 1st. September otherwise it must fail & untill that time it was intended the Troops should be stationed on the frontier to relieve the distresses of the Inhabitants from the cruel depredations of the savage daily committed on them, therefore you must see the necessity of your setting of[f] with your Regiment as soon as possible & to be expeditious. I am really ashamed to be seen in this Town so long, now near a month when our time is so short. If Waggons can be procured I would have them to carry the necessary articles up as far as Ft. Pitt, or wherever the troops are to be Stationed untill they march on the expedition. The Congress, board of War &c go from this next Saturday.
    I am yours &ca.

                    Valley Forge 7 [?] Augt. [?] 177[8][20]
    Nath. Ewing Commissary Genl. of Hides, informs me that it is the Custom, to weigh Hides just [?] as they were taken off the Beef witht. Horns, & Scull the Skin & the small [?] hoofs of the feet & sold to the Tanners from 2d to 4d per pound but is risen now to 2/. or 2/6 per lb Calf Skins sold formerly from 2/. to 2/6 per pound & now perhaps 8/ or [several words illegible]
    He Exchanges premium Hides for [remainder of page illegible] upon an Average of 1-1/2 pounds Say 1 lb upper and 1 lb Soal leather will make one pair—wch. is got for 13 lb raw Leather as above Raw Hides weigh from 30. to 100 lb wt. or 50 or 60 wt upon an Average
    Mr. Ewing proposes: that in future the Issuing Comisarys of the respective Brigades send the Hides of the

Cattle Slaughtered by them to the Commissary Genl. of Issue, & there, deliver them to the Commissary Genl. of Hides his Deputys or Assistants taking their Receipt for the Same—that the Brigadiers who can effect Exchanges for Stores, Draw upon the Commissary of Hides who will be bound to deliver such Hides to any Amot. of such Exchange [remainder of page illegible]

Memorandums 13th. Aug. 78[21]

Get Provisions as soon as possible down to F. Pitt, especially Flour. As many Boats as possible made & mended imediately. Court of inquiry on all the Meat before it is removed.

Write to Gov. Henry immediately by Colo. Gibson or Campbell for 50. or 60. Horse Men, & 1200. Foot without Delay.—from the nearest Counties to make up 1500. men as we have not above 300. Contl. Troops

Write to Lockart to send the articles mentioned in a List to up [us?] immediately Gn. or Caml. [Gibson or Campbell?]

Get from Col. Steel what he has procured, & what he has here or can get Soon, as Lockharts Must be regulated by that.

And also to hurry Morgans[?] flour & Liquor here, & see it done

Move the Men from Vanmitters to the Fort at buck Bottom

Write to Colo. Gaddis [at] Monongahela.

Encourage Volunteers from every quarter.—procktors[?] Regmt.

Inform the Lts. of Countys the posts will be abandoned the 1st. [of] Septr. next unless they keep them up at their own, or State Expence.

qd: Forts Randolph & Henry.

Man Fort Pitt by Heths Comy. & Militia from Capt. Roliter. 8 Miles of[f] from Fort Pitt along the Road

To Mo. of little Plumb Creek.	7 Miles
To Mo. of bigg plumb Creek.	5
To Mo. of Pockety Creek.	8
To Kiskaminatis Creek	12
To Kittaning	15
Miles	47

Remmember his Fort [?]
also To relieve Fort Henry 28th. Augt. wth. amunition, Instructions about Boats flats &ca.—to Scout & report to me daily—one to Command the whole—or great part &ca. &ca
Remmember Lead & powder above all.
Employ all the Armourers to get all the Guns &ca. in order.
Enquire what Number of Cattle & Horses are got.
Fort, & Stores Beaver Cr: 25. Miles for 400. Men.
ditto, do. at Beaver Town Muskingum 70. or 80. M.—500. Men
ditto, do. at Mohickons To. between 40. & 50. Miles—[blank] Men
ditto, do. at Sandusky, between 40. and 50. Miles—[blank] Men with Cannon if possible.
Qd: if it would not be better to errect Stockades, in a direct Line at 25 miles distance from each other, all the way, from Mo. of Beaver Cr; to Sandusky, which is 150. Miles No. 65. W. & would make 6 Forts—besides Beaver.

- - - - - - - - - -

Accot. of the Provisions Sent forward With the Army Under the Command of the Honourable General McIntosh, on the 4th of Novembr. 1778.[22]
Vizt.
340 keggs flour Estimated at 85 lb. each is 28,900 lb
332 Baggs ditto   do   at 140 each is   46,480
                                           75,380 lb
692 head of Cattle Estimated at
  300 lb each is   207,600 lb
42 keggs Salt Estimated at 3/4 of
  a Bushel each is   31-1/2 Bushl

Fort McIntosh Novr. 8th 1778
Sir
 I have had the honour of seeing your letter of the 7th Inst. to Col. Campbell, which has induced me to furnish you with this Return of the provisions sent forward with the Army, by which you will find that the qu[antity] exceeds one hundred Weight to each horse. As you have [words torn out] and I can assure you that both the keggs [words torn out] above [words torn out] estimated Somewhat [words torn out] than their re[gular] Contents. I am very happy to

find tha[t they] are able to furnish you with another Supply at any moment you may require, as will Appear to you in my letter of Yesterdays date by Col. Boyer. 132,000 lb of Flour is Certainly on this side of the Mountain, Ninty thousand of which now lys at this place, & our Consumption will not exceed 4 & 500 lb per day as the Pack horse men &ca are dispersing fast. I have furnished two horse loads of Turnips & Potatoes—which I hope will arrive safe with you. When you stand in need of Candles, please to Call upon Mr. Johnston the Commissary, Whom I have furnished with a Box full for the use of the General & field officers. I wish you every happiness that the Nature of your Situation will admitt of and has the honour to [be] with every mark of respect

        Sir Your most Obed. Sert.
    [Signed] John Irwin
Endorsed: To the Honorable General McIntosh

- - - - - - - - - -

A Return of the strength of the different Garrisons & Posts west of the Allegany Mountains under the Command of the Honorable Brigadier General Mckintosh 1st of January 1779.[23]

- - - - - - - - - -

"Expences Travelling to Fort Pit 1778—Account of Expences to Camp"

The United States   To Lachlan McIntosh—B.G.

		Dols.
1st.	To Board & Lodging at Geo. Stakes in Yorktown from the 30th. May to this Day while attending on Congress & the Board of Warr his Rect.	720.
	To Cash paid in York for Maps, pasting & Cases for them per Rt.	21.
13th	To Cash paid James Pollock at Carlisle for Board & Lodging while we stayed there getting necessarys ready for the Western Department & waiting Colo. Brodheads Regt. for Lancaster	94.54
	Dollars	835.54

34   LACHLAN MCINTOSH PAPERS

	Commissioned Officers						Staff							Non Commissd.		Rank & File
	Field Officers			Commissd. Officers												
	Colonels	Lieut. Colonels	Majors	Captains	Lieutenants	Ensigns	Chaplins	Quarter Masters	Pay Masters	Surgeons	Mates	Q. Master Serjeants	Serjeant Majors	Serjeants	Drums & Fifes	
Fort Hand				1		1					1			2		23
Fort Pitt				3	5	1				1	1		1	12	5	143
Randons Bottom																7
Fort McIntosh	1		1	5	1				1		1	1	1	36	13	385
Hollydays Cove						1								1		9
Fort Henry				1		1								1		25
Fort Randolph													1	5	1	42
Fort Laurens	1		1	3	2	4				1	1	1	1	17	4	136
Total Strength of the Westn. Army	2		2	13	8	7			1	2	4	2	4	74	23	770

1779
April
26th To Cash paid for Expences upon
the Road from Pittsburgh to Camp
in the Jerseys per Rects. 795.84

       Dollars 1631.48 [sic]

(To Cash I paid for two felt
Hatts for a)
To a Beaver Hat I gave an Indian
Chief will cost to Replace it 160.

           1791.48

To Ballance carryed to the Debit
of L M's Accot. 2008.42

        3800. Dollars
            [sic]

    Cr.
1778 By Cash recd. of the
   Warr Office on Accot. 1500

[Jan]y By two Horses bot. of
19 D. Q. M Genl. in
   Lancaster, he says
   Cost £ 300   800

1779
[Fe]by. By Cash recd. of Mr.
5th Boynton D. Q. M. Genl. of
   the Western Dept.
   on accot.   1000

April By ditto of ditto
2d. on accot.   500

        3800 Dollars

1779 To Pay as Brigr. Genl.
May 15th. in Contintal. Service from 15th.
    May 1778 to this Day is 12
    Mos. at 125 Dols. per is 1500

To ballance due upon my Ration accot. from the 25th October. 1777. to 7th April 1779. per accot.
6270 Rations at 1/3 Dollars each   2090.

                              Dollars 3590.
        Cr.
By Ballance of Money in
my Hands   2008.42
        Ballce. due L. M.   1581.48
        - - - - - - - - - -

The United States   To L. M.   Dr.[24]
    1779
    April   90
    8th   Paid at Colonel Nevills   2
    10th Paid for one Bushel Partain [?] 12
    9th   do. Mrs. Cook Yough
          [York] County   7
    12th do. Paid Peter Everley   8
    do.   Paid for Grog two Bottles   4
    12   Paid Doughertys   26   45
    do.   Paid Richard Hall for
          Grain & hay   38
    13   Paid Tomlinson for
          Grain & hay &ca.   31   75
    do.   Paid Mrs. Graig   19   45
    15th. Paid at Old Town   7
    do.   Paid Mr. Barnheart   26   45
    do.   Paid Guy Snow at Warm Springs 9
    do.   Paid Mrs. Yats for dinner   8
    16th. Paid Mr. Stogden Watkins ferry 16   30
    17th. Paid Michael Belchiser   28
    do.   Paid Scott for Gr   17   30
    [torn] Paid Mr. Gattes   61   30
    do.   Paid for Cyder royal 4 Quarts 5   30
    do.   Paid Samuel Cannada   11   60
    19th. Paid Adam Gardner   59   75
          Paid for Quart Beer   30
          Paid Samuel Boyd   14   45

20th.	Paid Wm. Ross in Lancaster	34	45
	Paid for Grain & [illegible]	18	
—th.	Paid Volentine at the Ship	25	60
	Paid George Webb for breakfast	8	60
	Paid Waggoner Sorrell horse	45	6
	Paid at the White horse for Drink	2	
21st.	Paid Caleb Way	9	60
		556	21

McIntosh to John Twiggs
Camp at the Brick Kills, Friday Morning
17th Septr. [1779][25]

Dr. Sir,

General Lincoln has ordered a Cessation of Arms between our Troops & the Enemy untill further orders.—therefore you are to be very carefull that none of your Men will fire a Gun upon them or go near the Enemys Lines untill you have Leave unless you should be attacked by any of their parties first.

At the same time you are to observe the Directions I gave you Yesterday, to Scout well from McGillivray's House upon Savannah River, to Old Oat's plantation upon Deveaus Swamp near our Camp, to Cut off every Communication with the Town which is your Station till further orders. I am Sir

Yours &ca.
[Signed] Lachn. McIntosh, B. G.

Colo. Twiggs

"Printed Parole agreeable to Capitulation"[26]

[May 1780]

I do hereby acknowledge myself to be a Prisoner of War upon my Parole, to his Excellency Sir Henry Clinton, and that I am thereby engaged until I shall be exchanged, or otherwise released therefrom, to remain within the bounds of Colleton County So. Carolina agreeable to the fourth Article of the Capitulation which secures my Property from being Molested by any of the British Troops as Long as I observe this Parole and that I shall not in the mean Time do, or cause any Thing to be done, prejudicial to the Success of his Majesty's Arms, or have any Criminal Intercourse or hold Correspondence with his Enemies; and that upon a Summons from his Excelleney, or other Person having Au thority thereto, that I will surrender myself to him or them at such Time and Plaee as I shall hereafter be required. [Copy on the back in McIntosh's hand]:

"I do hereby acknowledge myself to be a Prisoner of War upon My Parole, to his Excellency Sr. Henry Clinton, and that I am thereby engaged until I shall be exchanged or otherwise Released therefrom, to remain within the bounds of Colleton where my Plantation Lyes, agreeable to the Articles of Capitulation which Secures my Property from being Molested by any British Troops while I observe this Parole. And that I shall not in the Mean time do, or cause anything to be done, prejudicial to the Success of his Majesty's Arms, or hold any criminal Intercourse or Correspondence with his Enemys."

Declaration of Officers of the Georgia Line
Respecting General McIntosh.[27]

Whereas it appears that Congress have received a Letter said to be from Wm. Glascock Esqr. Speaker of the House of Assembly of the State of Georgia, Containing the following paragraph, "It is to be wished that we could advise Congress that the return of Brigadier General McIntosh gave satisfaction to either the Militia or Confederates, but the Common disatisfaction is such, & that founded on weighty reasons, it is highly necessary that Congress would whilst that Officer is in the Service of the United States direct some distant field for the exercise of his Abilitys." And also another Letter said to be from Governor Walton Containing the following paragraph "I am also ordered to apologise to Congress for the trouble given them respecting General McIntosh & to assure them that a General & setled aversion has & does prevail, I do not mean to suspect the Integrity of this Officer (for personally I am very much his friend) when I say it is the practice of Nations not to continue any Officer longer than he preserves the Confidence of the people."

We the Subscribers, Officers of the Georgia Continental Brigade think ourselves in honor bound to declare, that the said paragraphs, are in our opinions unjust, ungenerous, & malicious attacks upon the Character of General McIntosh who we think every way undeserving of such Aspersions, as from experience we have found him to be the brave, the humane, and the Circumspect Officer & the tenacious Citizen nor do we wish to be Commanded by any Officer in the Contl. Line in preference to him, And we further declare that no opinions or assertions of ours could ever give sanction to the above paragraphs, for had our Ideas of General McIntoshs Conduct been consulted & followed they would have conveyed to Congress that Officers Character, in diametrically oposite Colours to what it has been by the said paragraphs.

Given under our Hands at Augusta, the 17th. Day of May 1780.

[Signed] Jno. McIntosh Lieut Col. 3d Geoa. Regt.
John Lucas Captain 4th. Georgia Contl. Regt.
Geo. Handley Captain 1st. Geoa. Contl. Battn.
Nathal. Pearre Lt 3 B.
Elisha Miller Capt. 2nd. Georgia Continl. Battn.
Patrick Walsh Capt. Georgia Cont. Dragoons
Fras. Tennill Lt. 2d Contl. Battn.
Patk. Fitzpatrick Capt. 4th. G. B.
Arthur Hays Lieutnt. 4th C. Battn.
Christopher Hillary Lieut. 4th. Geo. Battn.
Henry Allison Lieut. 2d C. Geoa. B.
George Melven Captain 4th Georgia Battn.
John Frazer Lt. 3 G B
Laban Johnson Lieut of the Artillery
John Peter Wagnon Lieut. 3rd. Geo. Regt.
Thos. Glascock Lieut. 1st. Geoa. Battn.
Jesse Walton Lieut. 1st. G. Battalion
Wm. McDaniel Lt. G. Continental Lt. Dragoons
John Meanley Lt 3 G C Bt
Cornelius Collins Lieut. 2nd. Geo. Cont. Battn.
Wm. McIntosh Captn. 1st Geoa. regiment
Wm. Jordan Lt. 4th G. B.
Brossard Captain in georgia line
David Rees, Depy. Judge Advocate
Wm. Matthews Comy of Musters

N.B. Those officers of the Georgia Line who have not signed this declaration respeg. General McIntosh are Prisoners in Charles Town, & on furlough in the State of Virginia.

"Capt. Rob. Cooke 19th. June 1780"[28]

Sir

    I send you three Days provisions for five hundred and twenty five men to be delivered your Quarter masters at the landing for which hope youl order them to send me a recpt. If any mistakes should happen beg youl Inform me and belive me shall take pleasure in seting them right any aplications from your side the river must come thrue you in writing and the Genl. will give you an answer

    I am Sir your most obedient Huble Servant
      [Signed] Robt. Cooke
          As Comy [Assistant Commissary ?]Prisoners Charlestown 19th. June 1780
Endorsed: Genl. McIntosh
      Haddrills Point

Petition of Inhabitants of Augusta.[29]

    To his Excellency, Sir James Wright, Baronett, Captain General, Governor, & Commander in Chief, in, and over his Majesty's Province of Georgia, & Vice Admiral of the Same.

    The Humble petition of the Inhabitants of Augusta, and Parish of Saint Paul in said Province and others now Residing there. SHEWETH,

    That your petitioners have for some time past Laboured under great Anxiety of mind, and considered themselves and their property much exposed to depredations, in consequence of the unsettled situation of Affairs in the back parts of this Province, and finding, that notwithstanding the arivall of a Detachment of his Majesty's Troops in Augusta under the Command of Lt. Colonel Brown, who they expected might have been Vested with sufficient powers to restore to your petitioners the long wished for Blessings of Peace and Security, will remain in the most disagreeable State of uncertainty & Suspence.

    Your Petitioners therefore, exceedingly desirous to be

restored effectually to his Majestys peace and protection, Humbly pray your Excellency would be pleased as speedily as possible to receive and restore to his Majestys peace and Protection the Inhabitants of the said Parish in general, by such ways and Means as shall appear unto your Excellency best calculated for the reEstablishment of lasting peace to this long distracted Country, & true happiness and prosperity to the distressed Citizens thereof. and your Petitioners as in duty bound will ever pray.
dated at Augusta 25th. June 1780.
Signed by 49. persons.—that are found already.

- - - - - - - - - -

"Copy of Letter to [Mrs. Sarah McIntosh]
per Flagg per Capt. Nash"
Barr[acks] Had[drell]s Pt. So. Car.
7th Augt. '80

I have not much satisfaction in sending an open letter yet I cannot avoid informing you by the return of a Flagg to Newbern No. Carolina that I have kept my health pretty well since I have been a Prisoner, the Limit of the Genl. Officers is the Little Parish of Xt. Church opposite to Charlestown which we cannot complain of, & we must confess that we have hitherto had a Sufficient allowance of good Salt Provision, but cannot boast of any Luxury unless it is a Little Fish we catch at times ourselves, which Serves also for amusement & a necessary Exercise.

I was very Uneasy that I could obtain no certain account for a Long time of the rout you had taken, all I could Learn was that you Left Cambden, which I was sorry to hear, as you could not be much more injured than you have been already. Travelling near three hundred Miles from home with so large a Family, & Little or no Conveniency I thought sufficiently distressing without attempting to fly further. I am however so far happy now as to hear that your self & all the Children are well in health & fixed at Salsbury in No. Carolina, where if you can make it out tollerably I could wish you to remain untill we see what time brings forth. Tell Lackie I charge him to Stay with you & give every asistance in his power to the Family an Indulgence which I think cannot be refused by any Officer who Commands the Southern Army. You & he may always inform me of your Situation by way of the Army Leaving your Letters open, & I am displeased that he has not done it before.

They have reestablished an Assembly & compleat Legislature in Georgia & among other Acts have passed one to disqualify & render incapable the persons therein mentioned from holding &ca.&ca. &ca.—with many other circumstances that I forget.—& promised to enclose List of the Names Mentioned in the Act[30] which was also forgot.

Endorsed: To Mrs. Sarah McIntosh
at Salsbury No. Caro:
per Capt. Clemt. Nash

- - - - - - - - - -

A list of the Continental Officers, Prisoners of War in South Carolina in the order they are to be exchanged. [1780][31] [See page 43-44.]

- - - - - - - - - -

Continental Officers to McIntosh.[33]

January 7th. 1781.

Sir

The Officers of the Battallion late Colonel Parkers with Such of Blands as are present, do declare, that they Served the most of the Campaign of 79 under the command of Brigadier General McIntosh; that they neither publickly, privately, Generally or individually, ever Manifested or express'd to the executive Council of Georgia or any other publick body's or Individuals, the most distant dislike to General McIntosh as a gentleman or disapprobation to his Comand as an Officer, but had every reason to be highly Satisfied with both.

that they had during their Service in Georgia been Acquainted with its most respectable Citizens, who together with the people in General made frequent & publick avowals of their Good opinion of the General; and appeared by their alertness to take the field when-ever the General directed, to place in him the Greatest Confidence as an Officer.

In justice to themselves they are obliged to declare, that so much of the letters addressed to Congress from Mr. Walton, Govr. & Mr. Glascock Speaker, of Georgia as mentions or comprehends the Continental Troops "Generally having a

	line	Date of Commis.	When taken &c &c
B. Generals 6			
1 Wm. Moultrie	S.C.	16th. Septr. 76	12th May 80 C.T.
2 Ln. McIntosh	G.	do.	do. Died
3 Wm. Woodford	V.	do.	do. Died
4 Charles Scott	V.	2d April 77	do. Exchanged
5 [Louis Lebique] Duportail	E.	17th. Novr. 77	do. Died
6 James Hogan	N.C.	9th Feby. 79	
Colonels 10			
1 Samuel Elbert	G.	July 76	March 79 B.C. in Virga.
2 C. C. Pinkney	S.C.	16th. Septr. 76	12 May 80 C.T.
3 Wm. Russel	V.	19th Decemr. 76	do. Paroled
4 Nathal. Gist	V.	10th Januay. 77	do.
5 Thomas Clark	N.C.	5th Feby. 77	do.
6 ———— Delannoy	E.	17th Novemr. 77	do.
[Laumoy, - de Mons ?]			
7 John Patten	N.C.	22d Novemr. 77	do.
8 John Nevill	V.	11th Decemr. 77	do.
9 William Heath	V.	30th April 78	do. Paroled
10 Bernard Beekman	S.C.	20th June 79	do.
Lt. Colonels 11			
1 Wm. Henderson	S.C.	16th Septr. 76	do. Exchanged
2 Robert Mebane	N.C.	26th. Septr. 76	do.
3 Arch. Lytle	N.C.	26th Jany. 77	do.
4 Selby Harney	N.C.	22d Novr. 77	do.
5 Burges[s] Ball	V.	17th Decr. 77	do. Paroled
6 Gust. B. Wallace	V.	20th [March] 78	do.
7 Samuel Hopkins	V.	19th [June 78]	do.
8 Sam. J. Cabell	V.	[15 Dec. 78]	do.
10 Jonathan Clark	V.	[10 May 79]	do. Paroled
11 John F. Grimke	S.C.	20th June 79	12th May 80 C.T.
7 ———— DeCambray	E.	13 June 78	do.

LACHLAN MCINTOSH PAPERS

Majors 13
1	Thomas Hogg	N.C.	19th October 77	do. Exchanged
2	Richard C. Anderson	V.	10th Feby. 78	do. Exchanged
3	[Ferdinand] Debrahm	E.	11th Feby. 78	do. Exchanged
4	John Habersham	G.	21 March 78	do.
5	David Stevenson	V.	4th May 78	do.
6	Wm. Croghan	V.	16 May 78	do. Paroled
7	John Nelson	V.	28th. Novr. 78	do.
8	Andr. Waggoner	S.C.	15th Decemr. 78	do.
9	Isaac Harleston	V.	30th Decemr. 78	do.
10	William Lewis	S.C.	10th May 79	do.
11	Ephr. Mitchell	V.	20th June 79	do.
12	Charles Pelham	G.	25 June 79	do.
13	Philip Low		[18 June 78]	At Ponpon, Georgia (sic)
	Thomas Pinkney			

Captains 14
1	Daniel Cuthbert	G.	[blank]	March 79 B.C.
2	Bayler Hill	V.	20th Septr. 78	6 May 80 Santee. Exchad.
3	G. John McRee	N.C.	16th April 76	12 May 80 C.T. Exchanged
4	Felix Warley	S.C.	24h. May 76	do. Exchanged
5	John C. Smith	S.C.	16th. Septr. 76	do. Exchanged
6	William Mosly	V.	13th Decemr. 76	do. Exchanged
7	Tilman Dixon	N.C.	5th Feby. 77	do. Exchanged
8	John Dandridge	V.	7th Feby. 77	do.
9	John Gillison	V.	17th Feby. 77	do.
10	William Johnson	V.	19th [mutilated] 77[32]	do.
11	Clough Shelton	V.	1st M[arch] 77	do.
12	George Melvin	G.	1st [March] 77	do.
13	John Pitt	V.	[mutilated]	do.
14	[Lewis] Celeron	E.	[1 April 79]	do.

LETTERS AND DOCUMENTS 45

Setled aversion to General McIntosh" are with respect to themselves utterly false & are convinced were dictated from principles that have produced the Highest Injustice to the General

The Officers Subscribed are with Great Esteem & regard the Generals

    Mo. obt. Hble. Servants
[Signed] Sa[muel] Hopkins Lt. Colo.
    Parker Capt.
    Ben Taliaferro Capt.
    Tarlton Payne Capt
    Beverly Stubblefield Lt
    Thomas Parker Lt & Adjt
    Baylor Hill Capt. Dragoons
    David Meriwether Lt.
    Sam Hogg Lt.
    Richard C. Anderson Major 1st Virginia Regiment
Endorsed: The Honble.
    Genl. McIntosh

- - - - - - - - - -

"War Office 18th July 1781"[34]
    War Office July 18th. 1781

Sir

The Board request you will favour them with a List of the different Continental Officers specifying their ranks, who have [been] sent from Charles Town to Philadelphia [under] the several flags of Truce in consequ[ence] of the late Cartel settled between General [torn off] and Lord Cornwallis; also an Account of [the amount] of Money which they have respect[ively paid] for their passages, or for which they stand engaged.

    I am Sir
    Yr. most obed Hble Servant
    By order of the Board
  [Signed] Joseph Carleton
    Secy.

Brigr. General McIntosh
Endorsed: (Public Service)
    Brigadier General McIntosh
    Philadelphia
    War Office

List of General Officers now in Continental Service — 1st January 1782. Philadelphia George Washington Esqr. Genl. & Commander in Chief

Names	State they are from	When appointed Brigadiers	When promoted	Occurrences
Major Generals 14				
1. Israel Putnam	Connect.	18th. June '75	18th. [19th] June '75	Super And.
2. Horatio Gates	Virga.	22d. do. '75	16. May '76	At home.
3. Wm. Heath	Mass.	22d. June '75	9th. Augt. '76	
4. Nathl. Green	Rho. Is.	1. March '76	9th. Augt. '76	
5. Wm. Earl Stirling	Jersey	9th. Aug. '76	19th. Feb: '77	
6. Ar: St. Clair	Pennsy.		19th. Feb: '77	
7. Ben: Lincoln	Mass.		19th. Feb: '77	Secry. at war
8. Mars: DeLafayette	France		12th. May '77	France
9. Robt. Howe	No. Caro.	1st. March '76	20th. Oct: '77	
10. Alexr. McDougal	N. York	9. Aug: '76	20th. Oct: '77	
11. Baron St[e]uben	Germany		5th. May '78	Inspectr. Gen:
12. Wm. Smallwood	Maryld.	23d. Oct: '76	15. Sept. '80	
13. Saml. H. Parsons	Connect	9th: Augt. '76		
14. Chevr. Duportail	France	15th. Novr. '77		Engr. Genl. France
Brigadier Genls. 19.				
1. James Clinton	N. York	9th. Augt. '76		
2. Wm. Moultrie	So. Caro.	16. Sept. '76		
3. Lach: McIntosh	Georgia	16. Sept. '76		
4. Hen: Knox, Art.	Massa.	27. Decr. '76		Artillery
5. J. Glover	Mass.	21. Feb:. '77		
6. J. Patterson	Mass.	21. Feb: '77		
7. Anto. Wayne	Pennsyl.	21. Feb: '77		
8. Geo. Weden	Virginia	21. Feb: '77		
9. Peter Muhlenberg	Virginia	21. Feb: '77		
10. Geo. Clinton Govr.	N. York	5. March '77		Govr. N. York
11. Edw. Hand	Pennsyl.	1. Apr: '77		Adjt. Genl.
12. Chas. Scott	Virga.	1. Apr: '77		Prisr. of War
13. Jedidiah Huntington	Connect.	12. May '77		
14. Jethro Sumner	No. Caro:	9 Jan: '79		
15. Isaac Huger	So. Caro:	9. Jan: '79		
16. Mordecai Gist	Maryld.	9. Jan: '79		
17. [James] Irving [Irvine]	Pennsyl.	[26 Aug. 77]		Lt. Corps
18. [Daniel] Morgan	Virginia	[13 Oct. 80]		Brevette.
19. [Moses] Hazen.	Canada	[29 June 81]		
20. [John] Stark.	Hampshr.	[4 Oct. 77]		

General Officers, killed, Died, Resigned or dismissed &ca.

Names	States they are from	When Appointed Brigadiers	When promoted	Occurrences
Major Generals 11.				
1. Artimas Ward	Massa.		18th. [20th] June '75	resigned 23d. Apr. '76
2. Chs. Lee	Virginia		18. [17th] June '75	dismissed
3. Philip Schuyler	N. York		19th. June '75	resigned
4. Jos: Spencer	Massa. [Conn.]	22d. June '75	9th. Augt. '76	resigned
5. John Sullivan	Hampsh:	22. June '75	9. Augt. '76	resign'd
6. Tho: Mifflin	Pennsilv.	17. May '76	19. Feb: '77	resigned
7. Ad: Stephens	Virga.	4. Sept. '76	19. Feb: '77	Dismissed
8. Benedt. Arnold	Connect.	10. Jan: '76	2 May '77	Deserted to the Enemy
9. Baron DeKalb	France		[15 Sept.] '77	Killed, 16. Augt. '80
10. Sr. Thomas Conway	France	13. May '77	[13 Dec.] 78	resigned
11. Richd. Montgomery	N. York	22. June '75	9. Decr. '75	Killed 1st. Jany. '76
Brigadier Generals 29.				
1. Seth Pomeroy	Mass.	22 June '75		Never Acted.
2. David Woorster	Connt.	22 June '75		Killed
3. Rieh. Montgomery	see above.			
3. John Thomas	Mass.	22 June '75	qd.	Died. [2 June 76]
4. Joseph Fry[e]	Mass.	10 Janry. '76		resigned 23d. Apr: '76
5. John Armstrong	Pennsyl:	1. March '76		resigned 4th. Apr: '77
6. And: Lewis	Virga.	1. March '76		resigned 15th: Apr: '77
7. James Moore	No. Caro:	1. Mar: '76		Died — 9. Apr: '77
8. Baron DeWoodtke	[Prussia]	16. Mar: '76		[Died 28 July 76]
9. John Whitecome.	Mass:	5. June 76		
10. Hugh Mercer				
11. James Read				
12. Chr. Gadsden				
13. Chev.: DeFermoy				
14. Fra: Nash				
15. Jam: M: Varnum				
16. J. O. DeHaas				
17. J. Cadwalleder				
18. Ebenr. Learned				
19. Jo: Reed				
20. Count Polaski [Pulaski]				
21. Ja: Wilkinson				
22.	DeBhore [Prud'homme De Borre]			
23.	De Coudré			
24. Wm. Thomson				
25. John Nixon				
26. Wm. Maxwell				
27. Enoch Poor				
28. Wm. Woodford				
29. James Hogan				

	M.G.		B.G.	Quota
Hampshire has had	1	&	1	2. Regts. Inf.
Massachusetts	5		10	11. Inf. & Art.
Rhod Island	1		1	1.
Connecticut	3		2	6. Inf: & Cav:
N. York	3		2	3. Inf: & Art:
				2. (Inf. Art: Cav. & Ar:)
Jersey	1		1	
Pennsylva.	2		8	9 Inf: Art: Cav: & Ar:
Delaware	—		—	1
Maryland	1.		1	5
Virginia	3		7	11 Inf: Cav: & Art:
No. Caro:	1		4	4.
So. Caro:	—		2	2
Georgia	—		1	1
Foreigners	5.		6.	

14. M. Generals 150 Dos. per Mo. or 1800 a Year	25,200.	Dollars
" 15. Rations each per day at 9d. per Ration	7,665.	32,865
20. Brigadiers 125. dollars per Mo. or 1500 a Year	30,000	
" 12. Rations each per day at 9d. per rato. is	8,760	38,760
Gens. 34. Besides Waggons Horses & Forage dollars		71,625.
	Stg.	£ 16,115:1/6

British, Generals	23.	Admirals	16.	& 24 super annuated
Lt. Generals	80.	Vice Ad:	26.	half pay
M. Generals	50.	Rear Ad:	19	
	153		61.	in the Year 1781.

- - - - - - - - - -

"Letter intended for Congress from the Genls. Moultrie & McIntosh on the promotion of Knox & Duportail"
[February 1782][35]

Sir,

By the promotions of the Honourable the Congress were pleased to make lately of three Junior Brigadiers over our Heads—We cannot conceive they meant to injure the Usefullness, the Reputation, or the feelings of other faithful and old Servants of the Public after all their Toils, Efforts and Sufferings from the beginning of this War to the happy & pleasing period we have now a prospect of and much less can we bring ourselves to think they mean any injury, slight or Reflection upon those States who unsolicited by us honored us with their Choice, & of which we are Citizens—who have sacrificed & Suffered more in the glorious Contest than all the other States put together, & will be the Boast of their posterity for ages—Yet as some, or all of these inferences may possibly be surmised, we hope that Congress will take our Claims into further Consideration, & begg Leave to mention the Reasons upon which they are founded and wherein we conceive ourselves to be Materially injured.

Altho the Congress undoubtedly have a right to reward extraordinary and Conspicuous Merit, we apprehend & find they have *done (exercised that right)* it rarely heretofore, that on the contrary they found it necessary to Cultivate & Cherish that Spirit of emulation for Rank & Honors Natural to Military Characters—and that the too frequent Convulsions in their Army upon this Account, induced Congress to Establish a standing & fixed Rule of Promotion by the Resolution of the 22d. February 1777[36] which was ever afterwards looked upon and held by Officers as their right while their Conduct was unexceptionable. By this Rule Rank was universally settled throughout the whole Army in the Winter of that Year & Commissions found to be obtained through Influence & Management to the prejudice of others were vacated. & A Board of all the General Officers in the Main Army the ensuing March 1778 met by the Authority of the Commander in Chief, & in Virtue of this Act, took upon them to Reverse the order of Appointments made in the most deliberate & formal manner by Congress themselves on the said 22. Feby. 1777, of the four Brigadiers of the Virginia Line, which was approved of, and confirmed by Congress in their Resolutions of the 19th. of the Same Month of March & all their former Commissions ordered to be Canceled, nor would Congress *alter (receed from)* this Act of Justice & Consistency afterwards, upon the application of Brigr. Weedon on the 18th. August 1778. This Rule therefore became so much a principle of Promotion in the Army that Congress found it necessary & thought proper to make it a perpetual & a Standing Rule thereafter, whether Officers were prisoners of war or not, by the Resolution of the 24th. Novr. the same Year. and consequently if an Officer at any time suffered another to be Advanced over him, (by whatsoever Interest or Authority), he became immediately Contemptible and of no further Use in the Army.

This is exactly *(precisely)* the predicament we are now thrown in. We are not Conscious of any Censure either of us have deserved in the Line of our Duty. We have on the contrary received the Approbation of the Officers, whom we had the Honor of Serving under, & of Congress. Yet while we suffered a painful Imprisonment Brigadier Smallwood whose Commission was Younger than either was promoted over (*above*) us. Brigadier Duportail tho still Younger was first Exchanged in preference of and afterwards promoted over us—and now when we have at Length been Exchanged, and had the pleasing prospect once more of being active in the Service of our Country, & the Honor to assist in finishing that War we have been Instrumental in bringing to this happy period, Brigadier Knox is appointed a Major General over our Heads also. whatever the Merit of these Gentlemen may be (for we cannot (*are loth*) suppose any partiality or favor in the Case) we begg Leave to ask, what opinion the Army, or indeed the World must have of us? after these implyed (we had almost said Direct) & repeated Reflections or rather Attacks upon our Reputations & Honor? we think it cannot be otherwise than appear as intended to render us Useless & Contemptible in the Army & to throw us out of it altogether, for, if we attempt to take any Command under this our present predicament we must be despised by the very Army who used to Respect us. Upon every Principle therefore of equity & utility; by the practice of other Nations, the Laws Established, & so often Confirmed (*ratifyed*) for the Regulation of our own army we conceive that we have a Claim from (*upon*) the Justice of Congress, and a Right to be restored to that Rank & Honor we have been deprived of. Altho Brigr. Genl. J. Clinton can not join us in the application we do not mean to preclude him & would not wish to hurt the feelings of any Officer where they are most Susceptible, that is His Honor by being promoted over him.

    We have the Honor to be Respectfully
                    Your Excellys. most obt. Hble Servts.
                      W. M. Brigr. Genl. [William Moultrie]
                      L. M. Brigr. Gen. [Lachlan McIntosh]

His Excellency
The President of Congress

Menzies Baillie to Robert Baillie.[37]

Londo. 30th Apl 1782

Dear Brother

I wrote a few lines last Packet acknowledging receipt of yours of 10 Jany last which gave me great pleasure being the only one I had received from you since 11th Octr. 1780 which gave me much uneasiness because I considered nothing cou'd prevent your letters coming to hand but the ships being taken, but now it is certain they have been otherwise Secreted, I wrote almost every opportunity. latterly my letters were very short, because I was assured that very few letters that were addressed to friends of Government were delivered, which sufficiently accots. for your not hearing from me. I was prevented writing you by Mr McIver from Portsmouth, the Grand Fleet were under sailing orders & I had a large sum to pay of Prize money which required constant Work, if they had not been paid before the fleet sailed there woud have been a Mutiny, & before I had finished paying Mr McIver sailed. In the present situation of Publick affairs I hope my letters will be more likely to find their way, but 'till I am certain of that I shall not write you so fully as I woud otherwise do for it Vexes me exceedingly to write so many very long and Circumstantial letters on diffcrent matters all to no manner of purpose. I Inclose a Copy of Your Case in the loss of the goods & the Hero with the Attorney Genls opinion it does not appear you have received any of those sent out formerly. Mr Jno Tunno gave you the best advice how to have acted in those goods you shoud have let the Capt put them on Shore & taken them under protest; that held the underwriters bond. Your taking them from on board constitutes the delivery & exonerates the underwriters owners &ca Simpson has been too officious & pressed the Capt to do what he has done. I think you have recourse both on him & Count d'Estaing, but am afraid youll make little of them. As to appointments in the Civil line there can be none 'till matters are settled. A Series of misfortunes since the Commencement of the American war seems to depress your spirits. I do not wonder at it, but now it is over matters will soon come round, & I hope you'll soon get to your own Plantation & enjoy it more than ever. give yourself no uneasiness about your debts here, you shall never be called upon either for principal or Interest, there is no Sale for lands either in America or the West Indies, nor even for Estates in Scotland or England at 16 years purchase. I wrote to Sandie about 10 mos. ago I have had none from him these three years. I observe George is gone to an Attorney in Savannah which I hope will answer, his & the education of the others must suffer much it is a loss no time to be delayed in redeeming. I have frequently wrote to know if you designed any of them for the mercantile line, & if it suited any of their dispositions, it is unlucky when boys are put to a business their genius is not adapted to. John you say Inclines the army, that I think nothing of, it is the business lads first Chuse & first tire of, & the poorest business I know, however if he is of a Volatile lively disposition & has that strongly in his head he will settle to no other, if otherwise I'll take him or any of the others you think most adapted for the Merchantile line, & do them all the Service in my Power, but unless the lad has abilities, steady, of a solid settled disposition good tempered & can give unwearied application & can bear confinement he'll tire of it in a few years & think it a Task in place of a pleasure. You are the best judge which [of] them it will suit. I do think parents shoud always Chuse for their children unless the boy shows a strong genius and desire for some particular art. I shall expect to hear from you as soon after you receive this as opportunity offers & that you'll send John, or the one you think most calculated for a Merchant first Vessel or Packet. Brother James writes "desire Robt. to give out any small sum that he judges proper to that Vagabond Gillies provided he has taken up himself & can be of any Service to his Children, & to take his receipt, that he has recd. the money from Mr Alex Gillies writer in Edin[burg]h by Robts Hands & send over that rect. to you & I will get the money from his Brother here, but desire him not to let Gillies know that his Brother has ordered him to do any thing of that kind but that Robt has done it out of sympathy to him & is to make tryal to see if his Brother will advance any little thing to him when in distress" You'll make such use of that information as you do Judge expedient. I shall write you

next Packet but shall not trouble you with long letters 'till I am certain of their arriving Enclosed are 2 letters I received soon after last Packet sailed. I heard two days ago from Scotland they are all well My kind Compts & best wishes attend you all I am with great Esteem & regard Dr Brother
     [Signed] Your affect. Bro Menz[ie]s Baillie
[Footnote on Copy 2]:

- - - - - - - - - -

          Londo. 30 June 1782
Dear Brother
 Above is a Copy of my last I was prevented writing you last Packet by the Influenza which disorder has been very General all over Europe I have Just received yours of 18 Feby last am very glad you have got better but you are greatly to blame in giving way to that dispondency which your misfortunes has drawn on you are not singular it is a general distress & not owing to your or their misconduct give yourself no concern for what you owe here, if your confessing Judgment to me will secure your property for you 'till Matters are settled so as you can make an arrangement of [incomplete]

- - - - - - - - - -

 "Collo. Bedfords Letter with Answer—1782"[38]
Sir
 Your Letter much su_____ [most of line missing] rite me [most of line mutilated and illegible] my Negro Before me, it is true we intended to Carry a gerle but she would not have ben in the inside of yr. Waggon as I no of, I had Provided a Horse & Sadle for Her to ride, and Perhapes if you are acqunted with me a Twelve Months you wonte Catche me in a Lie. If I understand your Letter you Perpose to send your Waggon for Corn,—you no that I told you that I sold my Corn & Bacon and Every other thing that I culd well spare to the French,—but on Condition you would oblige me in your Wagon I would Spare you Six Barrils & more if it pd. Seasonable. I have Considered that I am not under any Obligation to spare you any Corn tho I have ordered for you to have it made into good Flower. If I shuld Find [remainder of letter torn off or illegible]

McIntosh's reply.

[First words torn off] of two Hours only—you told me your Brandy was better than 3 year old & I afterwards made you confess it was but 1-1/2 year.

One Lye.

You promised me in your Room by ourselves, Six barrels Corn immediately, with 300 lb flour—and if the wa[ter] did not fail your Mill, that you had a prospect of Supplying me all the Season, for which you would take Grain in Return when I got my Crop in, as I told you I had no Cash to pay you. & you Said, on consideration of my being a Stranger here—and all this, while I positively told you I could not Spare my Carravan, & before you expected to get it.—but afterwards *at parting,* so much seeming Generosity induced me notwithstanding the Inconveniency to tell you, that "I believe you must have the Stage Waggon, if you would put it in Compleat order at Petersburg"—All which if Compared with your Letter will be found to be—Another great Lye.

- - - - - - - - - -

State of Georgia[39]

We whose names are hereunto subscribed & seals affixed Commissioners appointed in & by an Act of the legislature of the State of Georgia passed at Augusta on the 4th day of May last past, for attainting th[ose] Persons & Confiscating the Estates real & personal of certain persons in the said Act named, Do acknowledge to have received from James Habersham of Savannah in the State of Georgia aforesaid his Bond bearing date the [2d] day of July last payable to his Honor John Mar[tin] Governor & Commander in Chief of the State of Georgia & to his successors in Office with condition there under written for the payment of the sum of thirteen hundred & Eighty seven pounds ten Shillings in Specie on or before the 2nd day of July [next in] the year of our Lord one thousand seven hundred and Eighty nine [several words illegible] Bond with sufficient security thereto bearing date on the said second day of July last past payable as aforesaid with condition there under written for the payment of Interest [at] the rate of seven pounds per Centum per Annum Yearly every year on the said sum of thirteen hundred & Eighty seven pounds ten Shillings until the said 2nd day of

July which will be in the year of our Lord one thousand seven hundred and Eighty nine which said Bonds we acknowledge to be as a Security & in full satisfaction for the consideration [of] purchase money of the several plantations & or Tracts herein after mentioned, that is to say, all that & those [Tra]ct or Tracts of Land whereon is two Settlements on the R[iver S]avannah late the property of Thos. Flaming [Flyming] whereon the [said] Flaming resided, containg. 1500 acres sold to the said [Hab]ersham at public vendue, with every thing there on an[d] to the same appertaining, also all that & those the Tract [of] Land chiefly pine land on Savannah River at or near T[ucke]seking containing one thousand acres late the property of Jno. Gr[aham ?]; also all that & those the Tract of Land late the property of James Herriott [or Harriott] containing two hundred & fifty acres all & every [part] of which Tracts of Land are situated in Effingham County [in] the State aforesaid. and we do hereby for Ourselves [and] the Survivors of us Commissioners as aforesaid Covenant and [ag]ree to and with the said James Habersham his Heirs & assigns [th]at we will on a reasonable demand to us made by him [illegible] as soon as circumstances or the event of War will [per]mit, make & deliver to the said James Habersham his Heirs & assigns a good & sufficient Title by conveyance in fee simple of all & singular the said lands & appertenances, he [or] them paying for the drawing & procureing to be maid or drawn such sufficient [illegible] conveyances, & we do [one line illegible] survey of the said three Tracts of Land [consis]ting of the supposed quantity be found that it shall & may be lawful for the said James Habersham to claim & demand a deduction from the said principle sum of thirteen hundred and eighty seven pounds ten Shillings at the following rates, (Viz) fourteen shillings [words missing] pence per acre for any deficiency in the Tract of 1500 [acres la]te the property of Thos. Flaming, eight shilling per acre for any deficiency in the Tract late Gr[aham] [line and a half illegible] being the prices at which said land [word illegible]
[Given under] our hands and seals at Savannah this the [illegible] 1782
               Signed by Seven Commissioners [not listed]
Signed [?] & delivered
in presence of [blank]

"Rough Estimate of the Civil List of the United States"
Civil List of the United States (1782)

Resolves of				
	3 Ministers Plenipotys. at £2500 Stg. each.		33333-1/3 Dols.	
	3 Secretarys each	£1000 do	13333-1/3 46,666-2/3	
	Financier, say	4000		
	Assistant, say	1850		
	1st. Clerk	1000.		
'80. 25 Sept.	under Clerks (say 4)	2000.	8,850.	
	Comptroler, say	2500.		
25 Sept.	Clerks (suppose 3)	1500.	4,000.	
	3 Auditors, at 2000.	6000		
25 Sept.	Clerks (say 6)	3000	9.000.	
	Register, suppose	1500		
25 Sept.	Clerks, say 2	1000	2,500.	
	13 Commissioners, 1500	19,500		
25 Sept.	13 Clerks a' 500	6,500	26,000.	
1780 13 Sept.	Secretary of Congress	2000.		
	do. D. Secretary, say	1000.		
25 Sept.	Clerks (suppose 3)	1500.		
13 Sept.	2 Chaplains at 400	800.		
	do. Messenger & Door-keeper	800.		
'80 14 Oct.	Secretary to Presdt. of Congress	450.		
	do. Steward to ditto	550		
[illegible word]	Presidents Table &ca &ca	8000		
	Stationary House Rents			
	Firewood, &ca for Offices	8000	23,100.	
13. Sept.	Treasurer, qd. if Contd.	2000		
	Clerk (say 2)	1000	3,000	
	3 Judges of Appeal	4500	Duty on	
	Register	1000	Captures	
	Clerks (say 2)	1000	6,500	
	Treasurer of Loans	900.		
	Clerk	500	1,400	
	Post Office. nothing & will yield a profit.			
	Interpreter & Translator	600		
	Printing & Charges	1400	2,000	
	Secretary at War	4000		
	Assistant do.	1250.		
	1st Clerk	1000		
	Under Clerks	2000	8,250	
	Secretary of Marine &ca.		8,250	
	Secretary of Foreign Affs. &c.		8,250	
The Embassadry brot. down			46,666	
			157,766	
	For Commissions		2,234	
		Dolls.	160,000 Total	

Civil List of the Internal Govermt. of Pennslyva. for 1780 is
nearly   30,000 Dollars
The other 12 States supposing them equal, which is a
great deal too mch.   360,000
                        390.000
The Unites States   160,000
per Annm.   550,000 £123,750 Stg.
which makes 12d. Sterling per head if evenly Divided among 2,475,000 Inhabitants. but Duty properly laid would Discharge the whole without any Taxes, Quit Rents or any Incumbrance.

Military Establishment Feby. 1782

14 Major Generals 166/	27,888	makes ½ pay		13,944
each 15 Rato. is 547½	7,665	35,553		
20. B. Generals 125/	30,000	½ Pay		15,000
each 12 Rato. at 9d.	8,804	38,804		
50. Colo. Infy. 900. An:	45,000	½ Pay		22,500
6 Rations each	10,950	55,950		
50. Lt. Colo. Infy. 720 Ann:	36,000		—	18,000
5 rations each	9,125	45,125.		
50. Majors of Infy. (600)	30,000		—	15,000
4 Rato. each day	7,300	37,300		
General & Field Officers exclu. of Forage		212,732		84,444
450 Captains of Infy. 40 Dols.	216,000		—	108,000
3 Rations each	48,450	264,450.		
1100 Subalterns 20-27 Avera[ge] 30.	396,000		—	198,000
3 Rato. each	80,300	476,300		
50 Regts.-Officers of Infantry		953,482		390,444
Besides 4. Regimts. of Dragoons				
4. Regimts. of Artilly				
2. Partizan Corps	Guessed			
1. Regmit. of Artificers	1/3 upon			
1. Corps Engrs. & Sappers		313,827		130,138
& the Hospital	Amot.			
& Staff Departmts.		1,271,309		520,582.

- - - - - - - - - -

"Extract of the General Assembly in favour of Genl. McIntosh 19th. July '83"[40]

House of Assembly July 19th. 1783.

The Committee to whom was Recommitted the Memorial of General McIntosh, Reported, and after some Amendments made thereto, was Agreed to by the House, and is as follows.

That as it appears to them, the General has lost most of his Vouchers by the Incidents of the late War, in Confidence of his veracity, such Charges in the Account Annexed to his Memorial as relate to Monies Advanced and Debts Con-

tracted for and on Account of the State or Continent; together with his Amount of Pay and Rations and Forrage, be allowed, the same being first duly Attested, and that the Auditor be directed to Audit and Pass the same, Seperating and distinguishing, Such State and Continental Charges agreeable to his Instructions and that on Certificate thereof by the Auditor Should the General require it, the Amount be deducted from any Purchase he or his Son Capt. William McIntosh has made, in Consideration of Considerable Sums in Money, many years since by him Advanced for the Service of the State, the other Charges being Losses of the General although the Committee are well convinced they are very great and have proceeded Chiefly from the early Active and decided Part he took in favour of his Country, yet as they make Part of a General Question, Your Committee think Cannot at this time be taken into Consideration.
Extract from the Minutes
[Signed] John Wilkinson C. G. A.

- - - - - - - - - -

We the Subscribers wishing to do Justice to our Country as Freemen do declare *George Walton* (a person lately appointed in a Seat of Justice) to be a *Coward and a Villain*, and are determined that if he (*George Walton*) attempts to take his Seat as chief Judge, that We the Subscribers will assist in pulling him of[f] of a Bench which ought to be filled with an Unblemished Character.
[Signed] Wm. McIntosh Jnr.[41]

- - - - - - - - - -

"Defence of Capt. William McIntosh—before a
General Court Martial—1783"
Mr. President—and Gentlemen of the Court.—
Few men attempt the Road to Glory and Fame without meeting with rubs & interruption from Seoundrels in their way.—altho I am a very Young Man yet, and may not be possessed of the prudence, or timmid Caution of more experienced, or Artful Men, I have been in the Military Service of my Country since the beggining of the War, and the first attempt to bring any charge against my Honor (which I defy the World to Sully) lies now before this respectable

A Return of Officers of the Georgia Line of the American Army entitled to Promotions by Resolve of Congress the 30th September 1783

Names	Rank	date Commissd.	time of Service & other Occurrences
1 Samuel Elbert	Colo. 2d Regt.	5. July 1776.	derranged Decr. 1782 when the Regiment was reduced to four Comps.
2 John McIntosh	Lt. Colo. Commt.	3. April 1778.	
3 John Habersham	Major	1 April 1778.	Continued during the war
5 Philip Low	Major	18. June 1778.	deranged in 1780.
4 Joseph Lane	Major	2. April 1778.	deranged by Resolve of 1780
6 Isaac Hicks	Captain	3. July 1776.	Retired since 1780.
7 George Handley	Captain	19. Octob. 1776	Retired in 1782.
8 John Bard	Captain	Novr. 1776	Retired since 1779.
9 John Lucas	Captain	1. March '77	during the war
10 Geo. Melvin	Captain	1. March '77	derranged in '82
11 Daniel Cuthbert	Captain	12. June '77	Prisoner during the war
12 Monsr. Brossard	Captain	26. June '77	in France
13 Emmanl. Peter Delaplain	Captain	26. May '77	in France during the war
14 Jos. Day	Captain	20. Sept. '77	Prisoner during the war
15 William McIntosh	Captain	17. Sept. '77	in service during the war
16 John Milton	Captain	15. Sept. '77	Retired in [blank]
17 Gideon Booker	Captain	24. Jany. 78.	derranged in 1782.
18 Lachlan McIntosh	Lieutenant	'77	during the war
19 Frans. Tennill	Lieut.	20th June '77	during the war
20 Littleby. Mosely	do.	20. July 76.	retired 1780.
21 Thos. Glascock	do.	1. July 77.	during the war

Court—a Court that know, that feels the Value of it & therefore I trust the sacred deposit [of it] in their hands with confidence—and it must appear the more extraordinary to you Gentlemen, as it is a Charge of *interrupting* that very police in my Native State, which I have been supporting, and Contending (*risquing my life*) to Establish for near Eight Years past, a consideration alone, that I am confident (*flatter myself*) you will think sufficient to shew the futility of it.—but I do not rest the Justification of my Honor upon this foundation alone (*only*)—my malicious prosecutor, and the principle evidence against me, Doctor Brownson, who Officiously interferred in this Affair, which he was in no way concerned in,—and is only the mean *Instrument*, or *Tool* of G. Walton—strains hard in his Evidence to prove the ar[t]ful Charge made out *between them* against me, of *interrupting the Civil Police*, & ungentleman[l]y behaviour—yet upon closer Examination, and cross questioning of him, he discovers the Cloven foot, and cannot help acknowledging the business of the Court, or Civil Police (according to his own Phrase) was over, & done before this happened—that the Chief Justice was then, only plain G. Walton, walking the Street, with half a dozen of his friends, like any other Man, when he was Corrected suitable to his Demerit, and is evident & known proven to the whole Town that he expected it, as I was under Solemn promise to give it to him before he was put into any Office, the first opportunity I had, & Conscious himself how much he deserved it.—Mr. Brownson, further confesses, that altho curiosity led some Young Gentlemen to see at a distance what was going on, that no other person but myself meddled with G. Walton.—that I made use of no other Instrument but the Horse Whip, which I must confess was well Laid on—without interruption from himself, or any other person untill he run into (*quite through*) the Gate—and that I had no other Weapon, but what I usually wear, & belongs to my Profession which I was determined not to disgrace by using it on such an Occasion—and yet this very formal Doctor Mr. Brownson, who deserves a Little of the same discipline with the Advice of his Prompter, to deprive me of Evidence, Artfully contrived to involve, two young Gentlemen, who do honor to their Age & Rank in the Army in the same Charges with me, altho he well knew, if they had no other intention more than mere Curiosity, it could be only to quell any qd [questions?] to prevent such Meddling busy Bodys as himself from interfering, in so Necessary a Chastisement (*or giving any unfair play.*)—and afterwards with the same Art had one of them released from his Arrest.—this may suffice, without taking up the Time of the Court, with any remarks upon other Evidences which nearly all amount to the same thing—I presume & flatter myself upon the whole it will appear Clear to you Gentlemen, that the Charges against me, are altogether false, groundless and absurd—that it was not the Chief Justice Officially, but simply the person of G. Walton, covered with infamy, instead of the Glory that should surround the office, that was so deservedly Corrected, after refusing to give Gentlemanly Satisfaetion for the most infamous behaviour that no part of the Civil Police, or business of (the Court) his Office, was in the least interrupted by it, and that no Gentleman would deserve that Name who could Act otherwise, after his refusing to give the Satisfaction usually required (*expected*) from persons who assume that Character, before he Tryed in Vain [to] Skreen himself under the Sanction of Office, for the most infamous of Crimes—*which are* so notorious & generally known that I need not repeat them.

But Supposing Gentlemen this Ideal Phantastical Charge a charge so laughable that none but a Pettifoging Lawyer could invent of *interrupting the Civil Police*, could be proved against an Officer in the Army: what does it amount to?— or how far does should it extend?—the Civil Police includes (*comprehends*) all the Civil Officers &ca. in a State, from the Governor downwards—common or ordinary, as well as Chief Justices, with all their Subordinates also to the Lowest Constable and surely all and each of these cannot have a Sanction to insult or injure their fellow Citizens who are not in Civil office like themselves, with impunity—or if it is only the Gentlemen of the Army who Ventured their Lives so often & Sacrificed their whole time for the freedom of our Country happily obtained, that must bear, & put up with ill treatment from any of them for fear of being brought to a Court Martial for some such new invented offence as *interrupting the Civil Police*, we must become the most despicable in the whole Community, for our Service & Lyable to continual Insults—for my own part I candidly confess & I think I speak the Language of every Member of this Court when I say that I cannot, nor will not put up with such, from any person living—my Commission or my Life are not equal to my Honor—nor does Congress require such Humiliating Conditions from us—a Cringing fawning Officer who ought to have Spirit is the most insignificant & despicable of all Characters (*Creatures*).

The only Law Books I am versed in Gentlemen are our Articles of Warr by them alone I am now to be tryed.—& I find no such Crime in them all, as *Interrupting the Civil Police*. The 1st. Art. of the 2d. Secto. which I suppose my accusers had in View to dragg in upon this Occasion, punishes traiterous or Disrespectful words against the *AUTHORITY* of Congress, or Legislature of any of the United States—which is exceeding proper, & was, when these Articles passed, the best Criterion & description of the Friends to the old Government, and those who differed with us altogether in essentials & Principles—as they struck at the root at once of our Independence, or our Authority as the Article emphatically expresses it & therefore unsafe to retain them, such men, in the Army.

But all the affected sophistry of Dr. Sangrado[42] with the Chicanery of his Counsellor cannot Strain this Article or any other to reach any difference that may happen between Individuals tho' often tryed—attempted to depress the Spirit of the Army.—and if this Shift fails them, as I am Confident it must, the second part of the Charge founded upon it, will fall of Course.

The Law of the State gives the proper redress for all Offences of this kind & that are not purely Military, but they would not Venture it in Savannah, where the general Voice approved of the Correction as richly deserved & the next Grand Jury whch. sat there had G. Walton suspended from his Office as unworthy of it and I look upon (*cannot help thinking*) it an Insult to the Honor and Judgment of my Brother Officers, that they should expect a better fate to their farcical Tryal from a respectable & Solemn Court Martial, &c which besides the obligations binding on all other Courts have their honor to Consider &c

Questions you are to ask of the Evidences, especially when you find any of them prevaricate, or desirous of hiding any part of the Truth

Vizt.—Can you say upon your Oath—or do you realy think, the Chastisement you say you Saw me give G Walton, was given him as Chief Justice,—or for his own infamous and personal behaviour to my Father? I could wish a direct Answer.—

The Answer—comes here—

Did you ever hear or know, that I was under promise before G. Walton was Chief Justice to Horse Whip him the first time I saw him out of his House—that I always carryed a Whip for that purpose,—and that he kept close in his House for that reason, untill he went then to the Court House for the first time?

The Answer—

Did I interrupt Mr. Walton in the Duty of his Office.— or, was it before, or after the Business of the Court was over, and finished, that this affair happened,—was it in a House or open Street?

The Answer—

Can you recollect the Names of the persons walking with G Walton in the Street at that time?

The Answer—Dr. Brownson, Mr. W Maxwell Mr. B. Lloyd, Seaborn Jones &ca.

Did G Walton or any of the Gentlemen with him make any opposition?—or how did they behave?

The Answer—

Did Lieutt. Ducoin,—Lieut. Stewart of the Horse or any other person offer to Join or asist me?

The Answer—

Had I any other Weapons at the time, than the whip, & the Sword I always wore,—or did you see me attempt to make use of anything but the Whip?

The Answer—

Had Lt. Ducoin, or Lt. Stewart any other arms, than the side arms they generally wore?

The Answer—

Did I come upon G. Walton privately, or in a public open Manner, & before his Face?

The Answer—

"Board of Claims Letter to the House. 1784."[43]

Sir,

The Board of Claims in compliance with (*at*) the desire of the Honl. the House of Assembly have laid their proceedings before the House, which they have hitherto kept to themselves, for reasons which must appear obvious to every person, as the Various Interests of Individuals will interfere with every general principle the Board have adopted & Laid down for the good of the whole, & will of course meet with opposition. I am directed Sir to inform the House that as so much Confidence has been placed in the Board, (at their first institution) who cannot have any separate views of their own independent of the Country they have endeavoured to the Utmost of their Judgments to discharge their Duty to their Country hitherto, and that if they are permitted to proceed in their own way without restraint or interferrence, they have in view, & flatter themselves they will (*may*) be able not only to Save the State from bankruptcy, and pay its Just Debts with honor, but also to make any Taxes hung upon the Citizens unnecessary which they apprehend is to be considered beyond the Interest of any individual.

I have the Honor to be Sir

Yr. most obt. Hble Sert.
[Signed] L. McIntosh P.B.
30th Jany. 1784

The Honle
James Habersham
Speaker of the Hle. the Ho. of Ass.

The Board to shew the necessity of Secrecy on some Occasions will take the Liberty to remind the Honl. House of the Celebrated Story of the Athenian Aristocles, who said in an Assembly of the people, that he had a plan in View of the utmost consequence to them, but in order to execute it, must be kept Secret from them, the people having great confidence in his ability, but afraid at the same time of his firery ambitious designs, left it to the opinion of his Rival Aristides surnamed the Just, who (altho the Secret is not [illegible word]) after it was disclosed to him, declared it was of the greatest benefit to the State but unjust for which reason to the eternal honor of that republic it was rejected.

The Board wish to know the determination (*opinion*) of the House on the business they are intrusted with, that they may determine whether they are to proceed or not.

With every mark of respect I have the Honor &c

Auditor's Office 20th: April 1784[44]

In the Settlement of Capt: William McIntosh's Account on the 31st: day of October last, he the said Capt: McIntosh gave Credit for the sum of two hundred and eighty three pounds for two Negroes purchased by him and for which sum the Continent is debited in my Books.

Also,

That in the settlement of his Brother Lachlan McIntosh's Accot. a Credit was entered for an old Negroe fellow, a Wench and Child, bought by the said Lachlan McIntosh for £141—but no sum extended; as the said Lachlan McIntosh had two valuable Negro Fellows taken and disposed of by the late Governor Martin at Augusta in the Year 1782, and for which he never received any payment or satisfaction.

[Signed] John Wereat Auditor

"Brother Jno. McIntosh 30th. August 1784,
Recd. 15th. Octob. '84"[45]

St. Thos. in the East the 30th Augt. 1784.

My Dear Brother

The 30th of last month, the Almighty visited the windward part of this Island with the most dreadfull huricane ever known by the oldest liver in short thiers scearcely a house standing, or any kind of Buildings in this & the next parish, & a number of lives lost with the Wrecks of Buildings as well as upon the Coast. Yet dreadfull as our Sufferings are upon the South Side, they felt very little of it upon the North Side as its force came from the No. East, my house being open to that Exposure was in a few minutes Blown down & every other Building & Tree in that direction Tore up by the Roots or Snapt off, in short my self & number of my Slaves was Buried in the Ruins of a Large Mass of Buildings I am now at a friends house Confined to bed ever since owing to the Bruises & Cold I got that dreadfull night their was little hopes of my Recovery untill 3 days agone, that it pleased God to Relieve me of part of my affliction, & altho' I have Reason to be thankfull that I was not Crush'd in the Buildings, Yet I find that I have lost my all even to my Wearing apperal & papers Excepting the lives of my few negroes & without a Speedy Supply of Provisions from the States of America they must die of famine; Yet what distresses me most at this Juncture is a letter of Credit your son John obtain'd from me, when he came from Georgia he came in a hurry to see me & told me he was to Return immediately that a Large Vessell with Lumber was stranded at Tiby & that his friends had purchased the Cargo for him & that the house of McLeans here had taken a Concern with him & had Charter'd a Ship to carry the lumber to this market where it was then much wanted, he said it was necessary for him to carry at least a Thousand pounds worth of negroes to pay for his part of the Cargo &c. I thought this Reasonable, & as he was immediately to Return with Such a Cargo cou'd Run no Risk. I gave him a letter to John McLean mentioning, as a Connection in Trade had taken place Between him & my Nephew I wou'd Join Either of them in Bond to a Ginuea house for a Thousand pounds worth of negroes for my Nephews Venture, in a Week after Giving this letter, I learn'd from him that the vessell they had in view was Charter'd by others & that McLean was wholly off & that he & Mr. Morison had Chartered a Schooner & begged I wou'd Come down & procure him some negroes as he was sure they wou'd chart 50 per Ct. upon them & be Back in 3 months at farthest I then went to Town & in his presence apply'd to the Guinea houses But they wou'd not go out of their old Tract & their money must be paid before any Remittance Cou'd be made from america Jack was so sensible of this that he gave up the thoughts of a venture in negroes & wrote me that he had more freight Engaged than the vessell Cou'd carry. it seems he fell in with a Mr. Gibbie who he knew was Consider'd here Lacking the solidity necessary to Carry men through life, this man proposed to him to carry my letter to friends of his & he wou'd procure him negroes as many as he wanted he immediately took £1086 worth of negroes from the house of Allans & Campbell & Bound me without my knowledge or Consent to pay for them in 6 & 10 months the day he saild he acquainted me with what he had done. Those Gentlemen through the interest of my friends have forbore to distress me untill now But finding that I have lost so Considerably in the Huricane they now say that they Cannot wait any longer But must have their money

What I have to Request of You is to make use of the authority nature has given You over him, take the negroes out of his hands & sell them without loss of time & Remitt the amount to the house of Allans & Campbell in Kingston. a letter from You letting them know what prospect they may Expect of payment may probably satisfy them for John has already deceived them & they will not Regard his letters. how soon I am able to get out of Bed will send You a power of attorney, Tho' I hope he'll be Ruled by You without. Gibbie pester'd me to give him & Doctr. Irvine a power against him & gave me Broad hints that Remittance woud not be made without I took such a step. I Rest wholly upon Your friendship to settle this Business with all speed. I am now so Weary & faint that I Can add no more save my most affectionate love to Your Wife & family & to all friends there & I am ever Your affectionate Brother

[Signed] Jno. Mackintosh

Endorsed:
 Brig. General Lachlan McIntosh
 at Savannah in the State of Georgia

- - - - - - - - - -

"Henry Emanuel Lutterloh 30th Dec. 1784 wth. Printed Advertisement."
     Charles Town South Carolina.[46]
     Dec 30th 1784.

Sir

The Honour I had to be acquainted with you, when we Lay at Valley forge where I acted as first deputy Quarter Master Genl. makes me take the Liberty to write to you, on a Plan which I have made in the Northern States to recover the unpaid claims against the Crown of Grt Britain and Persons acting under the Crown. The Northern States have given Us great Sums! and I thought it best to sent Major

Fuhrer on to North Car. & this State, but finding at my arrival here; That he has not been nor wrote to your State (where great Claims must be left unpaid); I thought it best to communicate the Plan to you, and to beg your advise & protection in the Establishing proper agents who would work under my Direction and collect the Claims upon the same Terms as others do with Us in Concern. The recovery of the Negrow's and devestation made on privat property is a great object, and can only [be] recovered by a Company of Men who will make it their business to Sue the right persons. We talked often together (if you recollect,) about procuring Settlers for your large Tracts of Lands, and No State can florish without great Numbers of Inhabitants and Trade & Taxes must be Supported by its Numbers. My being a Native of Germany and resolved to fixe in America, could give Me the best ways & means to bring over any Number of Settlers, if a State wants Some, and I should like to take a agency for that business at the same time I never was in Georgia & therefore cannot judge how Such a Plan would be Supported by the Assembly. Should be very glad to have your opinion on this Subject, having the Honour to be with great Respect

        Sir
        Your Most obed hble Sr.
     [Signed] H. E. Lutterloh

Charles Town
at Mr Hane
Broad Street
Endorsed: To the Honorable
    Major Genl. McIntosh
    at Sawana
Honord by Doct. George Tredway Junr.

The Public   to Lachn. MacIntosh   Dr. [1784]
 for Articles which the Auditor left unsettled in his former Account.
1777
 1. To my whole Crop of Rice (chief part
   of which was then cut) Corn, pease,
   Potatoes, &c. on the Ground in 1776. all

taken and destroyed by our own Troops, who burn't my Fences & turned their Horses into the field, which obliged me to remove my Family to Savannah—at least £500.
2. To the Crops of 1777, '78, '79, '80, '81 and '82, being Six years, all lost in Consequence of the removal of my Family, in which time they could make nothing 3,000.
3. To my Dwelling House, Barn & other buildings.—Dams, Trunks, Fences, and other Improvements, all destroy'd & gone to ruin in consequence of their being forced to remove—at least 1,500
4. To above 300 head of horned Cattle I had in 1775, & their Increase, with Hoggs Sheep & other Stock 1,200
5. To a Stock of breeding Mears & young Horses, of the Chickisaw Breed 250
7. To Furniture in the Country, Tools, Clothes, Books & Valuable papers, besides the Furniture I bought in Savannah which was all lost when the To. was taken 400
8. To 3 Riding Chairs & a Cart &ca. 100
6. To 24 Negroe Slaves lost & obliged to Sell in consequence of my removal at £75 1,800
Charged at £70.30 is £1680.
9. To Expences of my Family since they were drove from their Home in Decr. 1776 & during their Exile & Retreat, £200 per Ann. 1,200
  £9,950

[Page 2] Brought forward £9,950
10. To extraordinary Expences for myself during my Service, & in Captivity to support the Rank & Character of Continental Brigr. General of the State 1,800
11. To 10 Valuable Blooded Horses lost in the Service, some of which Cost 60

Guineas left to the Liberality of the House at £50 per hd.		500
		£12,250
Deduct for £5 each on 24 Slaves, being Charged in the Account rendered only 70 per hd.		120
		£12,130
The Auditor Settled for part of the Accout. the 22d. April 1784, as underneath, Amounting to		6,170.14.4
Amot. of original Accot. rendered		£18,300.14.4

1777
Novr. To Amot. of his Accot. from 13 Feby. 1776 to this date for his pay rations & a variety of expences paid by him per his Accot.   £6170.14.4
  deduct
Interest charged on the
Accot.   £1380.1.4
On the price of Horse charged £50 in the Accot. & I am Instructed to allow but £25   25   1405.1.4
           £4765.13

  Cr.
By Cash recd. from the Treasurers of Georgia at different times per his Accot. (no State of it being to be got from the late Treasurers) £2,500, in depreciated Money, Say on the Average of 1777, Vizt.
    1 Jany.   100
    21 Decr.   286.4
        386.4
(£ 1300.14/6/-is 193.2 per Cent   1293.19.11
   ballance per Audit   £ 3471.13.1

"Bror. Jno. McIntosh Letter of 30th Novr. 1785 per Greivis received 6th. Feby. 1786."[47]

Kingston the 30th Novembr. 1785

My Dear Brother

Being in this Town when Captn. Greevis [Grieve] arrived from Savannah I call'd upon him Expecting letters from You, & others of my friends there, the Captain to my great surprise told me he saw You a little before he Saild, but that You gave him no letters for me this astonish'd me, as I so often wrote to You of the Situation Your son John has reduced me to, desiring You wou'd use Your authority over him to do me an act of Justice. I wrote to You & himself by Mrs. Nathl. Hall who saild for Georgia some days ago setting forth that all my negroes, save 5 are in the Marshalls Custody for the debt he owes to the House of Allans & Campbell, of this Town Merchants, & are actually to be sold at Marshalls Sale the 1st. of March next for what Ready money can be Rais'd upon them without a Sufficient Remittance is made to discharge that debt before then, So, that I again urge, & Request You'll oblige him Either to dispose of the negroes he Carry'd over, or Return them with out money, or Produce can be Transmitted here for their amount without Loss of time, to save my negroes which are three times their value, But if sold at Marshall sale will not pay the debt which is £800 Currency. Messr. Allans & Campbell has deliver'd up Johns Bonds to me, upon my delivering up my Slaves, taking my note of hand to make Good any difficiency that might happen upon the sale of 47 fine Slaves, with their maintainance Goal fees &c. he is owing a Mr. Welch here about £1700, But as that was a Transaction of Trade between them apprehends, my Engagement from a motive of serving him only ought to be first attended to. he Wrote to the house of Allans & Campbell to Insure upon a Vessel that he never sent here for which they paid a premium of £70, which I cannot Recover from the Insurors, without he Sends a Certificate to satisfy them that, that vessell never saild for this Island John has put it out of my power to go to England last Spring to Recover my Eye sight. as the famous Barren Danzell was then in London, the first Oculist in Europe, & I had an introduction to him from a very near Relation of his who assured me that the operation would not Cost me a farthing, & that he wou'd pledge himself he wou'd Restore my Sight as perfect as ever it was in 14 days time, the hopes of so near a prospect of such a Blessing, made me happier than all the Wealth in the world wou'd have made me; but alas I have now only left the melancholly prospect of Spending the Remainder of life in the greatest indigence & Darkness without Your Exertions will oblige Your son to act uprightly by me for I am Sorry to Say, that I have very little hopes from his feelings without I hear from You in a Reasonable time, I'll be under the disagreeable necessity of sending powers of attorney over, or go myself for after the Sale of my Slaves I can have nothing to do in this Island.

I hope Yourself Wife & family with the Rest of my friends there are well: which will ever give me the greatest pleasure to hear. I beg I may be Remembered in the kindest & most affectionate manner to them. Doctr. McIntosh is well But his Brother. a Youth is dieng. a Lieut Wm. Fraser of the 42nd Regiment who is our uncle son by the Mother[48] is arrived here & desired his kind Complts. to You & I am

my dear Brothr.

Your most affectionate Brother
[Signed] Jno. Mackintosh

Endorsed:
General McIntosh
Georgia

"My Accot. against the Public for Indian Treaty"[49]
The Public   To Lachlan McIntosh   Dr.
1785.—for eleven Days attendance on the Governor
 & the Creek Indians at a Conference held
 with them in Savannah, with a Servant &
 Horses, at 4 dollars per day,   £10. 5.4
 for my own, & Servant & Horses time from
 the 20th. October when I left home to the 8.
 November when I left Galphington attending a Treaty there with the Creek Indians
 as a Commissioner from Georgia is 20 days
 at 4 dollars per day   18.13.4
               £28.18.8

State of Georgia:

This Indenture Tripartite made the first day of January in the Year of our Lord One thousand Seven hundred and Eighty Eight and twelf Year of American Independence. Between Lachlan Mckintosh Esquire late Major General in the American Army now of the County of Chatham and State aforesaid of the one (*first*) part, George Threadcraft Esquire[50] now of the same County and State aforesaid of the other (*second*) part, and William Mackintosh Junior Esquire son of the said Lachlan & late a Major in the Line of the American Army, now of the said County & State, of the third part. WHEREAS the said Lachlan Mackintosh is minded to settle certain Estates of Land herein after Mentioned upon his said Son William, for his better advancement in the World, and for the better Support of his Family should he think proper to Marry and should he have Children,[51] THIS INDENTURE WITNESSETH, therefore that the said Lachlan McIntosh for & in Consideration of the Natural Love and Affection which he hath and bears to his said Son William Mackintosh and for the farther Consideration of the sum of Five pounds Sterling to him in hand paid by the said George Threadcraft, the receipt whereof the said Lachlan McIntosh doth hereby Acknowledge and doth release, acquit and discharge the said George Threadcraft his Heirs Exors & Admors by these Presents HAVE granted, bargained, sold, aliened, remised, released and confirmed, and by these Presents DO grant, bargain, sell, alien, remise, Release and Confirm unto the said George Threadcraft and his Heirs (in his actual possession now being by Virtue of a bargain and Sale to him thereof made by an Indenture of Lease for one whole Year, bearing date the next before the day of the date of these presents, and by force of the Statute for transferring Uses into possession) ALL that improved Plantation Parcel or Tract of Land Originally granted to John Holmes for four hundred Acres, but contains only three hundred and fifty Acres, and was conveyed by the said Holmes to the said Lachlan McIntosh, situate lying & being in the Parish of Saint Andrew now in Liberty County in the State of Georgia aforesaid, and butting and bounding on the North West by Land originally granted to John Munroe, on the

North East by Vacant Lands, on the South East by Land of the said Lachlan McIntosh, & Lands still Vacant, & on the South West by Cathead Creek AND ALSO another Plantation Parcel or Tract of Land fronting the former Tract on the South West, and upon the opposite side of the said Cat Head Creek, to be laid out by a Line which is to run fifty degrees West of the South point, from the South West Hickory Corner Tree of the said Tract of three hundred & fifty Acres, upon, or near a high bluff of the said Cathead Creek, from thence in the same Course or direction over & across the said Creek, and afterwards continued in the same direction untill it comes to the Main branch of Shingle Creek, from thence down along the Stream or the ebb tide of the said Shingle Creek to the Mouth thereof & into the North branch of the Alatamaha or Darien River and down along the Stream or ebb tide of the said Darien River to the Mouth of Cat Head Creek aforesaid, and from thence up the said Cat Head Creek as the flood tide runs to the place opposite the said Hickory Corner the place of beginning, whatever the quantity of Acres of Land more or less which these bounds (*Limits*) may contain, it being the South East part of a larger Tract of Land originally granted to the said Lachlan McIntosh commonly called the point Tract situate lying & being in the said County of Liberty & State aforesaid & is a Neck of Land between the said Cathead Creek & branches of the said River Alatamaha, & bounded on the No. West by Lands granted to Mary McCulloch & Children As by a Plat of these Tracts of Land hereunto annexed as also to the original Grants may more clearly fully & at large appear.

AND ALSO a Town Lot No. 5. East Division, Ninety by one hundred & thirty feet, in the Town of Darien upon the River Alatamaha. Also a Lot sixty by Ninety feet in the Town of [blank][52] upon said River when laid out known in the plan thereof by the Number 74. Also a Lot one hundred by one hundred feet in the Town of [blank] on Doboy Island No. 1. East Division and ALSO the Lots No. 1 and 2 of 100 by 200 feet each Lot in the Town of Oglethorpe upon Saint Simons Island.

TOGETHER with all Houses, Outh Houses, buildings,

Improvements, Trees, Woods, Underwoods, Ways Paths Passages, privileges, advantages, emoluments, Heriditaments, & appurtenances whatsoever to the said Tracts and Lots of Land belonging, or Accepted known, held, or enjoyed as part parcel or Member thereof: and the Reversion and Reversions, Remainder and Remainders, Rents, Issues & profits thereof, together with all Deeds, Escripts, Minuments and Writings relating to the aforesaid Tracts & Lots of Land, Hereditaments & Premisses, hereby bargained & sold, or intended so to be TO HAVE AND TO HOLD the said Tracts & Lots of Land, Tenements hereditaments and appurtenances, and all & singular the premisses herein before Mentioned, and every part hereof unto him the said G. Threadcraft his Heirs and Assigns, upon such trusts, and to such Uses as are herein after expressed and declared, and to no other Use, intent, or purpose whatsoever, That is to say, in Trust to suffer and permit the said William Mackintosh Junior son of the said Lachlan & his heirs, or any of them whom he may appoint by his last Will if he shd. die to have, receive and take the Rents, issues and profits thereof, and to possess and Occupy the same for and during the term, or time of Twenty one Years, AND at and after the expiration of that Estate To the said G. Threadcraft his Heirs & Assigns in trust & Confidence that he or they will well and sufficiently Convey the said Tracts & Lots of Lands with all and singular the premisses and appurtenances, unto him the said William Mackintosh Junior his Heirs and assigns forever in fee simple if he shall be then Living or if he should die before the expiration of the said term of twenty one Years, then, & in that case unto the lawful Heir or Heirs of the said William Mackintosh Junior or any one or more of them whom the said William may direct, in his last Will and Testament duely executed and Attested if he leaves any (provided this Estate is not made Lyable for any debts contracted prior to the expiration of the aforesaid term of twenty one Years, or Alienated for any transactions before the end of that term as I conceive by that time the Possessors will begin to know the Value of it).

[What appears to be a second draft of the last part of this indenture is written on the back]:

To have and to hold the said Tracts & Lots of Land

&ca.—unto him the said G Threadcraft and his Heirs and Assigns (qd: forever) to such Uses, upon such trusts, provisions and Conditions nevertheless as are herein after Limitted, and appointed, of & concerning the same and to no other purpose whatsoever, that is to say, To the said G. Threadcraft and his Heirs, in Trust, To the Use of the said William Mackintosh Junior son of the said Lachlan, for, and during the term of his the said William's Natural Life, without Impeachment of, or for, any Manner of Waste &ca.—and from & after the decease of the said William To the said G Threadcraft his Heirs & Assigns in trust & Confidence that he or they will well and sufficiently Convey the said Tracts of Land with all & singular the premisses & appurtenances, unto the Lawful Heir or Heirs of the said William Mackintosh Junior or any one or more of them whom the said William may direct in his last Will & Testament duely executed & attested if he leaves any.

(this Estate not to be made Lyable for any Debts contracted by him in his Life.)

If he refuses to accept of or to pay Taxes for any of the said Tracts or Lots of Land upon these Conditions, such Tract or Lot shall go to any of his Brothers who will take them on the said terms giving a preference to the oldest

- - - - - - - - - -

Sir[53]

The Critical Situation of the Southern States, which, for a considerable length of time have been exposed to the ravages of war, and are become the object of reduction with the Court of London; pressed on congress to take measures heretofore, for baffling the Designs of the Enemy. It was hoped that the Events which followed the late Storm would have produced the means of an effectual cooperation of the force of our ally but your last letter stating Some difficulties beyond those which formerly appeared—we cannot, consistent, with a proper Sense of what we owe to our almost ruined country, omit, representing the necessity of having the enemy, immediately and effectually opposed in the pursuit of a Design, to accomplish which the greatest part of the british force has been employed in the course of the last two years.

When the natural Weakness of the Southern parts is considered, arising from thinness of population, and the destruction of the troops which formed the different Lines belonging to them, there cannot be a doubt of your using the desired measures to engage the force of our allies—the recovery of the Southern States, and the capture of the british would in our opinion contribute to a Speedy termination of the war, and indeed, it is to be presumed, that their Successes in Georgia & South Carolina could alone have furnished the british Court with a pretence of calling on parliament for the means of Supporting a War in America this year.

"My Letter to Mr. F. Courvoisie 23d. May '91
with an order on Capt. John Howell at Augusta"

Savannah 23d. May 1791

Dear Sir,

Inclosed I give an order in your favor on Captain John Howell of Augusta, for One hundred pounds in Specific Certificates, which I doubt not he will pay you when you inform him how much I am distressed at this particular time and that I have no other means of paying you my last Year's Tax.

I am Sir
Yr. obt. Hble. Servt.
[Signed] Lachn. McIntosh

Mr. Frans. Courvoisie

P.S. if Captain Howell can with more ease, Let you have two hundred pounds of Georgia Paper Money, it may Answer as well if you can exchange it.

Endorsed:
Frans. Courvoisie Esqr.
Savannah

List of McIntosh's Lottery Tickets, 1791.[54]

The marks and Numbers and Signers of fifty Lottery Tickets of the United States in 1776, first Class, in the hands of Lachlan McIntosh the elder, of Savannah, which were never yet enquired into, and the prizes (if there were any among them) never called for, and in such cases, by the original Scheme, were to be laid out for Tickets in the second and third Classes. The first ticket in this List is copyed at Length which serves for all the rest. VIZT.

m

United States Lottery   No. 98,152
Class the first.
This Ticket entitles the bearer to receive such prize as may be drawn against its Number, According to a Resolve of Congress passed at Philadelphia, November 18th. 1776
Z   J Barge

Y. No.98.153. J. Barge
A. No.98,154. J. Barge
X. No.98,155. J. Barge
S. No.98.156. J. Barge
L. No.98,157. J. Barge
K. No.98,158. J. Barge
F. No.98,159. J. Barge
E. No.98,160. J. Barge
Z. No.98,161. J. Barge

L. No.99,282. S. Delaney
K. No.99,283. S. Delaney
F. No.99,284. S. Delaney
E. No.99,285. S. Delaney
Z. No.99,286. S. Delaney
Y. No.99,287. S. Delaney
A. No.99,288. S. Delaney
X. No.99,289. S. Delaney
S. No.99,290. S. Delaney
L. No.99,291. S. Delaney
K. No.99,292. S. Delaney
F. No.99,293. S. Delaney
E. No.99,294. S. Delaney
Z. No.99,295. S. Delaney
Y. No.99,296. S. Delaney
A. No.99,297. S. Delaney

X. No.99,298. S. Delaney
S. No.99,299. S. Delaney
L. No.99,300. S. Delaney
K. No.99,301. S. Delaney
F. No.99,302. S. Delaney
E. No.99,303. S. Delaney
Z. No.99,304. S. Delaney
Y. No.99,305. S. Delaney
A. No.99,306. S. Delaney
X. No.99,307. S. Delaney

S. No.99,308. S. Delaney
L. No.99,309. S. Delaney
K. No.99.310. S. Delaney
F. No.99,311. S. Delaney
E. No.99,312. S. Delaney
Z. No.99,313. S. Delaney
Y. No.99,314. S. Delaney
A. No.99,315. S. Delaney
X. No.99,316. S. Delaney
S. No.99,317. S. Delaney
L. No.99,318. S. Delaney
K. No.99,319. S. Delaney
F. No.99,320. S. Delaney
E. No.99,321. S. Delaney

Fifty Tickets altogether, marked Numbered & signed as above.

Savannah in Georgia
4th. August 1791
[Signed] Lachn. McIntosh

"Jas. Seagrove Letter 3d. Decr. 1791"[55]

Dear Sir

Your favour by Godfrey in my Boat with the Corn you was so good as to send came safe to hand. Want of opportunity hath prevented my writing you until this time. I have now to request that you will have ready beat out 150 Bushels of Corn & if you have 100 Bush[el]s Cow Peas for which I will pay you he[re] by an order of Messr. Spiers McLeod & Co. in Savannah. I shall dispatch a Vessel Tomorrow morning for it and hope you will have it ready. Excuse this scrawl as the Bearer is very impatient

I am with Respect
Your obedt H Ser.
[Signed] Js. Seagrove
St. Mary's 3d Decr 1791

Majr. John McIntosh
Endorsed: Majr. John McIntosh
on St. Simons
To be forwarded by Mr. D. Manson as soon as possible.

"Subscription favor of John Houstoun Esqr. for £150."

Whereas John Houstoun esqr hath been appointed by the General Assembly one of the Judges of the Superior Court of this State

And whereas the Salery affixed to the said Office is conceived by us to be Inadequate. We the Subscribers do hereby promise to use our influence with the City Corporation to pass a Vote in favor of the said John Houstoun for £150 Sterling, in addition to the Sum of £350 allowed by the State, and in case of failure with that Body, We also promise to use every Means in our power to obtain the Said Sum in his favor in the General Assembly.

Jos. Habersham	Dav. Montaigut
Jos. Clay	Jas. Bulloch
Jas. Jackson	Jos Clay Jun.
John Brickell	Ben. Lloyd
Chs. Odingsells	Spiers McLeod & Co.
Rob. Bolton	Richd. S. Footman

Wm. Ewing—13
Alex Watt
Wm. pinder
Jno. Fisher
Chs. Jackson
H. Cuyler
Benj. Lindsay

John McIver
George Parker
Thos. Hogg
Saml. Beecroft
T. Netherclift
Wm. Lamb
Balthazar Shaffer
Sam Stirk
James Simpson
D. Mitchell
Peter Lafitte
John Moore
Ben. Sheftall Senr.
J. Betts
D. Sullivan
Wm. Clarke
Jona. Clark
Andw. McCredie
Mat Johnston
Rob. Woodhouse
Richd. Wall
Igns. Geohegan
G. Wilson
John Smith
J. Taylor
J. Bendix
Coachman Polack

F. T. Smithson
Fras. Watlington
Geo. Throop
John Habersham
Wm. Coales
John Currie—12
first page

Livy Abrahams
Wm. Parkman
P. D. Lieven & Co.
John Storie
his
Lucas X Lucenia
mark
Joseph Roberts
Wm. Moore
John Beatty
Edmond Dillon
Benjamin Leatch—37
Owen Owens
Wm. Brown
Jas. Clark
John Wreck qd:
Danl. Course
Isaac Course
Jas. Robertson
Jno. Love
A Mcqueen
Tho. Bourke
Ebenezer Jackson
Jas. Mossman
Leond. Cecil
Wm. Stephens

Jas. Chapman
Jas. Cochran
Jo. Day
Jno. P. Ward
J. Whitefield
Edwd. Wright
Thos. Elfe
Jas. Habersham
Js. Delaroque
D. McLeod
Jas. Mirrilies
Jno. Robertson
Mat. McAllister
Js. Seagrove
Jos. Abrahams
Wm. Reny
Jno. Wallace
John G. Williamson
Frs. Doyle
John Armour
Henry Putnam
Ben. Putnam—36
Abr. Leggett
J Hall
Wm. Vanderlockt
J. McGillivray—4

13
12
37
36
4
———
102

142 altogether

14. Jany. 1792

"Gideon Denison's Letter dated Savannah 26th.
Jany. '93 & delivered same day by
Billy Deveaux"[56]

Savannah 26th Jany 1793

Genl. McIntosh
Sir/
It is out of my power to furnish the negros to your *Satisfaction* & it is equally impossible to pay you egreeable to your wishes for the one half of the mortgage. I therefore must decline doing any thing farther in the matter than to reinstate Major Pendleton his asigns with full possession of the Mortgage, by he or they returning my Bond & note. I have notifyed John Berrien Esq who holds the Mortgage for the parties to that effect. any damage that you may sustain in consequence, I am willing to leave & submit to Judgment of indifferent men   I am Sir your ob. Sert.
[Signed] G. Denison

Endorsed:
General L. McIntosh
Present

- - - - - - - - - -

"Reply to a Bill in Equity"

STATE OF GEORGIA[57]	On the Equity side of the
John McIntosh Complainant	Superior Court
by his next friends	The Answer of Lachlan
Vs.	McIntosh one of the
William and Lachlan the	defendants to the Bill
e[l]der Esquires	of the Complainant.

This defendant being required by the Bill of the Complainant to discover facts relative to the estate of the intestate George McIntosh the Complainants father long before he had taken any part in the administration of it, and being willing in order to do every possible justice, and render every satisfaction in his power to the Complainant, to go into a narrative of the transactions of the estate as far as he can recollect, prior to his taking a part in the administration of it; at the same time saving and reserving to himself now and at all times hereafter all and all manner of benefit of advantage of exception to the many insufficiencies, uncertainties and other imperfections and defects in the Complainants Bill contained, for answer thereto or to so much thereof as this defendant thinks is any ways material or necessary to answer, he answereth and saith: That after the peace of Aix La Chapelle the latter end of the Year one thousand Seven hundred and forty eight, every resource this then young Colony now state of Georgia had for its support being withdrawn, it became almost entirely depopulated, that among other emigrants this defendant left his parents and went to Charleston South Carolina, where he carried his youngest brother the late George McIntosh the father of the Complainant, who was at that time about eleven years of age, put him to a grammar school at this defendants own expence, and after the said George had acquired such other accomplishments as were then taught at that place, this defendant bound the said George for four years to an Architect and allowed him one hundred pounds Carolina currency a year during the Term of his the said George's apprenticeship for pocket money, purchased a Negro boy for him to be brought up to the same business with himself, and to attend upon him, who is still alive, as this defendant believes and the most valuable slave belonging to the Complainant being the chief manager of his estate; This defendant further answering saith that after the term of the said George's apprenticeship expired, this defendant brought him back to Georgia and got him appointed Commissary of supplies for the Troops in garrison at Frederica, and other posts dependent thereon, instructed him in geometry and surveying and furnished him with books for those purposes, in order, that the said George might by those means acquire a more perfect Knowledge of his own Country and have an opportunity of getting the most valuable Lands at that early period for himself, as this defendant advised and directed him. And as the inclination of the said George soon after his return from Charleston led him to planting, this defendant, was also his security in Charleston for the first parcel of Negroes the said George ever purchased with which and his own industry he acquired all the property he ever possessed. Of all these advantages he made the best use and became one of the most thriving planters in this state, uniformly ascribing all his successes to this defendants steady friendships to him, and always declaring and looking upon this defendant in the light of a father and tryed friend, rather than a brother; And this defendant further answering admits it to be true that the late George McIntosh brother to this defendant and father of the Complainant did depart this life at or about the time mentioned in the Complainants Bill of Complaint, and that the said George died intestate and without a Will, to the best of this defendants Knowledge and belief: And this defendant admits it to be true that the Complainant is the only child of the said George McIntosh now living, and that the said George was at the time of his death possessed of a considerable real estate in Lands amounting to the best of this defendants knowledge to thirteen thousand and eighty acres, consisting of forty five tracts, situate in the different Counties of Liberty Glynn and Camden in this state, and also a Lot of land in Savannah, the Grants and Titles to which said Lands and Lot were on the third day of July in the Year one thousand seven hundred and ninety two delivered to the Complainant, by this defendant, as by his receipt appears. And this defendant further answering admits it to be true that the said George at the time of his death was possessed of a considerable personal estate, consisting of Negroes, and other things, but denies that there ever came to this defendants Hands and possession any more or other of the personal estate of the Intestate than the Negroes mentioned in the Inventory herewith exhibited and appraised at three thousand seven hundred and sixty two pounds on the ninth and eleventh of August one thousand seven hundred and eighty four, and on the seventeenth day of January one thousand seven hundred and eighty six and seventeen pieces of silver, consisting of spoons and other old plate which was neglected to be put in the appraisement and is kept as a memorial for the Complainant of his Parents whom he can hardly remember: And this defendant further answering saith that he was at Augusta when he first heard of the death of the Intestate that he immediately came down, but did not arrive until some days after his funeral, that the short time this defendant stayed at the habitation of the Intestate, he principally enquired and examined into his papers, which were scattered about and hudled into unlocked broken Trunks; but found none of any consequence except the Grants and Titles for the Lands before mentioned, which were all put carefully into a small portmanteau Trunk and secured by the defendants Wife and family, in a pursuit by the enemy of seven or eight hundred miles, while he this defendant was a prisoner in Charleston, being captured at the siege of that City, in the Year of our Lord one thousand seven hundred and eighty; And this defendant further answering saith that about the time he came down from Augusta after his brother's death he engaged a Waggoner to carry to Charleston to the care of Mr. Philip Minis since deceased a parcel of Indigo belonging to the Intestate which Indigo he never saw nor does he know the quantity but sent it there that it might be secured out of the reach of the enemy, and has since been informed and believes it was afterwards delivered to the order of Sir George Houstoun; all the personal estate besides of every description was in the hurry of the retreat from the common enemy left in the care of the Overseer on the Intestate's plantation at Sapello river. And this defendant further answering denies that he did immediately after the death of the said George apply for the administration of his estate to the Superior Court of this County, but admits it to be true that sometime in the Year one thousand seven hundred and eighty three after the evacuation of Savannah by the British forces at the solicitation of the late Sir Patrick and the present Sir George Houstoun he this defendant agreed to join them together with James Houstoun in the administration of the estate of the Intestate George provided they would give this defendant no trouble in the administration of it in pursuance of which solicitation and assent of this defendant application was made and Letters of Administration this defendant believes were granted to them accordingly on or about the thirtieth day of October one thousand seven hundred and eighty three, but this defendant denies that he ever qualified or acted under those Letters. And this defendant further answering admits that true it is that some time after the said Letters were granted if granted at all, to wit about the tenth day of December in the Year last aforesaid William McIntosh the elder a brother of this defendant and a codefendant to the Bill of the Complainant petitioned the Chief Justice of this state praying for a revocation of the Letters granted to the said Sir Patrick George and James Houstoun and this defendant and that the administration of the said estate and effects of the said Intestate might be granted to him the said William as eldest brother of the Intestate and to such others as by law or open consent might be entitled to the same, that the Chief Justice on considering the said petition granted the prayer thereof, and thereupon adjudged, that the administration of the Estate & Effects of the said Intestate of right belonged to the said William the petitioner whereupon he the said William without the knowledge or consent of this defendant had his this defendants name joined with the said William in the Judge's order for the Letters, but this defendant having shortly before that period returned to this state after an absence of near five years on being exchanged for General Ohara, his family then in Virginia and his affairs much deranged by the War which required all his attention in his advanced stage of life, refused to qualify or have any thing to do with the said estate for a considerable time, however on seeing the estate of his said brother George much neglected and wasted and being impressed with the necessity of his joining the said William in the Administration of it in order to save it as far as possible for the Complainant the only child and representative of the Intestate this defendant did on the twenty fourth day of May one thousand seven hundred and eighty four qualify with the other defendant to this Bill and take upon himself jointly with him the administration of the said estate. And this defendant further answering denies that he has acted as an administrator ever since the letters were granted because this defendant says that he never got possession of the Negroes of the said estate till about the first day of January one thousand seven hundred and eighty five. And this defendant further answering saith, that his only motive in joining in the administration was to protect the estate from waste and ruin, himself under the most embarrassing circumstances, incredibly poor after a long and necessary absence from his Country, plundered of almost every thing he possessed and not a farthing of money belonging to the estate on hand or any present means of making any, all the moveable effects belonging to the estate having been sold together with twenty two of the best Negroes by the late administrators Sir Patrick and George Houstoun under the usurpation, nothing to purchase tools cloths provisions or any other necessary for settling the Negroes without selling some of them, neither could credit be obtained, even if the means of settling them had been in the power of this defendant, the whole Country around was harrassed by a banditti accustomed to plunder and rob insomuch that there really was no safety for any moveable property twenty miles distant from Savannah and in addition to all this an Indian War shortly after broke out which nearly depopulated the whole Country South of Chatham County, under all those circumstances which this defendant believes would have terrified almost any other person than this defendant and the other from undertaking so arduous a task, they notwithstanding determined old and inactive as they were to persevere although no other means in their power were left than to hire out the Negroes to the highest bidder from year to year which was also attended with many inconveniences and much trouble and risque as the state about that period abounded with paper emissions of various kinds which served as a medium for cash in dealings amongst the Citizens, these circumstances coupled with the tediousness of legal proceeedings induced people to give exhorbitant prices for every article offered for sale notwithstanding which this and his codefendant under all these embarrassments had no alternative left but to make the trial, not supposing the Claimant whom they had so essentially served would endeavor to take advantage of any little inadvertencies or irregularities which they might have fallen into under such circumstances, and in such items. And this defendant further answering saith that some time after he qualified as an Administrator John Houstoun Esquire an Uncle of the Complainant instituted an Action against this defendant and the said William his brother as Administrators of the Intestate in the name of Miss Ann Stewart and recovered an account of three hundred and twenty two pounds seventeen shillings and three pence with interest thereon, and that the present Sir George Houstoun another Uncle to the Complainant after engaging Samuel Stirk William Stephens and John Houstoun Esquires had three writs served on these defendants on the same day as Administrators of the said estate for about two thousand pounds sterling with interest charged on that sum to the day of bringing the Actions which nearly doubled the original debt and at that time in this defendants opinion would have swallowed up the whole estate if sold for cash, at length after much expence which this defendant at that time could but illy afford and frequent attendancies in Court the fate of these Actions was by order of Court left to arbitration and instead of allowing the said Sir George the Sums of Money he demanded it was awarded that he should pay the defendants seventy eight pounds eight shillings and nine pence and return a young Negroe fellow the said Sir George detained and since sold for one hundred pounds as this defendant believes, and also pay them three hundred and seventeen pounds three shillings and five pence with interest from the first day of January one thousand seven hundred and eighty one as surviving Administrators of the said George McIntosh under the british usurpation, and the said Sir George should also use the utmost of his endeavors to recover ninety two pounds sterling due by his brother in law George Kincade for Negroe hire during the said british administration of the estate which this defendant believes to be still due as by the award will appear. And this defendant further answering admits it to be true that he together with his codefendant did on the twenty third day of December one thousand seven hundred and eighty four at Great Ogeechee where the Negroes of the said Intestates estate then were in possession of William McIntosh the Younger[,] son of this defendant to whom they had been hired for that Year by Sir Patrick and George Houstoun set up and expose to sale in pursuance of public notice given all the taskable hands of the Intestate consisting of twenty eight in number from the first of January one thousand seven hundred and eighty five till the first of January one thousand seven hundred and eighty six as by the said notice will appear when to this defendants surprise they were knock'd off at the enormous rate of twenty pounds for each taskable hand to this defendants son William which he this defendant much disapproved of as the said William was a near relation of the Complainant and had given so extravagant a price for the Negroes that he could never expect to pay their hire by labor but the said William persisted in his purchase, and this defendant further answering admits that the same Negroes that were hired to the said William his Son for the Year one thousand seven hundred and eighty five after being duly advertised in the Gazette of the twenty third day of December of that Year to be disposed of for the Year one thousand seven hundred and eighty six at Savannah the conditions of which were that the purchaser should give bond and warrant of Attorney to confess Judgment thereon within twelve months for the hire of the Negroes that Year as by a copy of the advertisement will appear, which this defendant thought might probably prevent his said Son William from getting them a second year were knocked off at the enormous price of nineteen pounds twelve shillings and six pence for each taskable hand to Richard Leake who immediately signed the conditions of sale in the name and on behalf of the said William McIntosh who was not present at the sale, this circumstance so much displeased this defendant that he hardly spoke to the said William, his son for several years. The Auctioneer after the sale according to the conditions thereof had the Negroes appraised made out the Bond and warrant of Attorney and presented them to the said William, but could not prevail on him to execute them who still had the Negroes in possession, thus the Auctioneer was put off from day to day as this defendant was informed and believes, by the purchaser until that Year was too far spent to advertise and sell them over again; And this defendant further answering saith that he repeatedly pressed the said William his son for a fulfilment of his agreement for the Year one thousand seven hundred and eighty five which he never fully completed as well as for the payment of his bond for the hire of the Negroes for the Year one thousand seven hundred and eighty four, and that he the said William frequently promised to discharge the greatest part if not the whole of the hire for the Year one thousand seven hundred and eighty four and one thousand seven hundred and eighty five when his crop should be beatten out which he said was delayed in order to get his land in order provided he was not sued for the same otherwise he would keep the estate out of the money three four or five years if possible.

This defendant thus awkwardly and delicately situated by the imprudence and obstinacy of his said Son William was determined to act against him with more decision than against any other person in a like situation and accordingly having received no rice or other payment agreeably to promise from his Son William he put the bond for the Year one thousand seven hundred and eighty four and agreement for the Year one thousand seven hundred and eighty five into the hands of James Jackson Esquire Attorney at Law on the twenty sixth day of August one thousand seven hundred and eighty six to be immediately sued Mr. Jackson was then the defendants only counsel in all the transactions of the estate and advised this defendant to defer bringing the Suit against the said William till the circulation of the paper medium ceased as there were persons watching this defendants conduct who would not hestitate saying that he sued his Son William in order to favor him and to afford a pretence of paying the debt in paper money which was much depreciated and continued to be a legal tender till the Guardians of the Complainant received the whole of the property of the Intestate and the sole direction of it out of the hands of this and the other defendant. This defendant further answering saith that in order to avoid the evils and incoveniencies of the years one thousand seven hundred and eighty five and one thousand seven hundred and eighty Six and finding that nothing could be made out of the Negroes by hiring them, he with the other defendant to the Bill ventured for the Year one thousand seven hundred and eighty seven to place them on the plantation of the Intestate situate on Sapelo river although the Indians were still troublesome but without tools seed rice necessaries of any kind or money of their own or of the estates, in this unavoidable dilemma they were obliged to send two of the Negroes to Savannah to be sold, but as no more than twenty five pounds was offered for each, they were brought back again and wench called Polly who was the wife of a fellow belonging to Lachlan McIntosh the younger was purchased by him for fifty six pounds to be paid in corn, rough rice and seed potatoes which necessity obliged the defendants to accept without having time to advertise her according to law whereby the rest of the Negroes were relieved otherwise they must have been sent adrift for a subsistence and all prospects of a crop given up, the necessary delay occasioned by these circumstances, with the bad order of the land laying waste for many years, without the necessary buildings and other accommodations required on a rice plantation reduced this years crop to eighty barrels of rice with the necessary provisions. And this defendant further answering admits that in the beginning of the Year one thousand seven hundred and eighty eight there was a fine prospect of a crop, but that early in that year the Indians began to kill and plunder slaves and other property all around the neighborhood of the plantation which necessarily obliged the defendants to be at the expence of keeping a guard of white men constantly over the Negroes rather than loose so promising a crop, and for the further security of the Slaves which was still a greater object with the defendants than the crop itself they purchased a large Pittiagua boat to carry off all the negroes at once to the Islands in case of any dangerous alarm which so frequently happened that the crop this year neated only forty eight barrels which barely paid the heavy expence attending the culture of it. And this Defendant further answering saith that the Year one thousand seven hundred and eighty nine was attended with nearly the same expence and trouble with the Indians, yet the Crop neated ninety eight barrels of rice and plenty of provisions, seed rice and seed potatoes, as by the account hereto annexed and exhibited to this honorable Court will very clearly and regularly appear, all of which were in the beginning of the year one thousand seven hundred and ninety delivered to the Complainants Guardians together with all the Slaves mentioned in the Inventory except a Wench Polly sold for provisions as before is mentioned and a fellow called Billy who after being advertised according to Law was sold to Patrick Crookshanks for fifty seven pounds who gave his note payable in [blank] days from the date thereof which was put in Suit and Judgment obtained thereon which this defendant says is now of force the reasons for selling this Negroe were because he was an idle fellow and a runaway and has since as this Defendant has been informed and believes shot in the woods. And this Defendant further answering saith that the debts dues and demands in favor of and against the estate of the Intestate as far as they have come within his knowledge will appear by the accounts hereto annexed and exhibited to this honorable Court and which he prays together with the other Accounts attached to them may be considered as part of his answer to the Complainants Bill. And this Defendant denies all and all manner of combination and confederacy wherewith he stands charged in and by the said Bill of Complaint: Without that, that there is any other matter or thing material or necessary for this defendant to make answer unto, and not herein and hereby well and sufficiently answered unto confessed or avoided, traversed or denied, is true. All which matters and things this defendant is ready to aver and prove, as this Honorable Court shall direct and award, and hereby prays to be hence dismissed with his reasonable Costs and Charges in this behalf most wrongfully sustained.

       [Signed] Matt. McAllister Solictr.
           for Defdt L. M.
           10th. Septr. 1793.
       [Signed] Lachn. McIntosh

Sworn to this 11th. Septr. 1793 Before
[Signed] J. Houstoun

    John Steele to Lachlan McIntosh.[58]
        Treasury Department
        Comptroller's Office
        March 13, 1800

Sir,

By recurring to the 2d. section of the Act of the 2d. of March 1799, you will perceive that the time therein prescribed for receiving the statements of the Emoluments and Expenditures of the Officers of the customs for the year 1799, has elapsed, and as you have by neglecting to comply therewith, rendered yourself liable to the penalty provided in said Act; unless satisfactory reasons are offered without delay, I shall feel it my duty to institute suit for the recovery thereof.

         I am, Sir
         very respectfully
         your obt. servant
     [Signed] Jno. Steele

Lachlan McIntosh Esquire
Endorsed: Lachlan McIntosh Esquire
     Naval Officer, Savannah Georgia
Postmark: Comptroller's Office
    (Signed) Jno. Steele
Stamped: FREE

"A Calculation of the real instrinsick Value of
Lands in Georgia." [Not dated]

A calculation of the real, intrinsick Value of Tide Swamp Land, in the best Pitch of the Tide, and Lyable to no hazard, being deemed the most Valuable Lands in the States of Carolina & Georgia.—where the Interest of Money is Seven per Centum per Annm.—and upon the supposition which cannot now be doubted, that real Estates there, are as permanent & sure as any where else.

150. Acres of such Land (being independent of Reservoirs &ca.) makes what is commonly reckoned a compleat Rice Plantation, sufficient for the direction of one Manager (& when in order is the best Land for Indigo Provision &ca.) grows better the Longer it is wrought, and will produce three barrels containing 550 lb. Net Rice annually to the Acre (altho some have made five barrels) is 450. barrs. at £3 Sterling per bbl.   £1,350

Such Plantation will require 35 able Slaves to Manage it, which have been Usually hired in Carolina and Georgia at, or under £10 each per Annum, which paid the purchaser of the Slaves a very good Interest. But to include all Expences & every exigence that may happen we will say 40. Slaves at £12 each per Year is   480

The Net Annual produce   £ 870

The Net Annual profit therefore of 150. Acres best Tide Land when in order is Eight hundred & seventy Pounds Sterling, or £5.16/. per Acre forever clear of all Charges.—which at fourteen Years purchase, equal to Seven per Cent. Interest, is worth £80 Sterling per Acre. Say Eight pounds Sterg. per Acre.

Note, the hire of Slaves is prefered above for the easier Calculation & least risque, altho' purchasing of them would make the Expences of the Plantation less in the End.

It ought to be observed also, that in Europe where the Usual rate of Interest (which governs all Contracts) between Individuals is 5 per Cent. or twenty Year's purchase—that real Landed Estates there sells for thirty, forty, & fifty Years of their Annual Income, because Money is continually depreciating in Value as it increases in quantity.—while Landed Estates for that very reason proportionably Appreciates or rises in Value.—& is moveover a surer & more improvable Property.

- - - - - - - - - -

John Mackintosh to Thomas Tebzum[59] [?]
Thos Tebzum [?] Esqr.   [No place or date]
Sir
    Since I wrote my last w[hic]h was yesterday I am informed that the market for Oak at Philadelphia is dull in which Case I hope youll order the Cargo to the most Eligible place as a delay woud occasion much inconvenience—but as I trust entirely in you & Capt. Hunter I need not say More I Remain With Much Esteem
                                            Your Ser
                                [Signed] J. Mackintosh

- - - - - - - - - -

Fragment of a return of stores, date and place missing.

Poultry	Wheel Barrows	Feet red bay Boards	Valuation in Sterling at the Market place in Savannah
	12	175	£ 2004
			3810
			4841
			6403
			9507

- - - - - - - - - -

END OF PART I

PART II
Journals

"Part of G McIntosh's Journal"[60]

20th very busy in prepareing for my Journey, Stoped in to Genl. McIntosh's abt. 9 oClock. Soon after the provt. Marshals Deputy came with a Note Directed to G. M. desiring my Body to be immediately delivered to him. Such a suden and unexpected Note surprised me much and went out of the Genls. House directly to enquire about Town what such a suden demand was for. I was soon inform'd by a Gentleman of undoubted vorasity that the Govr. & Council had Resolved in a private manner to send me with one Col. Ferrel, a man of an infamous character, and 20 men in the most ignomeneous manner they could to Congress, and soon after I was informed that Ferrel intended carrying me in Irons thro the Continent, which report has since been confirm'd by Capt. Nash who Col. Ferrel dispatched after me being inform'd in N. C. that I was on my Way to Congress. Such proceedings in the Govr. & Council alarmed me very much after what they had promised me the monday before which made me determine to keep out of there way for a little time to see if they would reconsider my case and permit me to go as they had first promised with Capt. Scott & another Gentln. and wrote a letter every three or four days to that purpose another motive I had in writing was to Let them know that I had not Left the State, as I had been twice in the Marshels Custody. I was Certain my security's had nothing to do with me, but the Bond had not been taken up from the Marshel, they thought then to come upon the Security's notwithstanding they had siesed all my Estate. I then sent to all my Security's informing them of my intention to go to Congress without their Guard or Leave provided they had no objection, as it was all along my own intention & request to them to Let me go to Congress to clear my character, which will appear by the Resolve of Council which enlarged me on Baile. all that I could see or hear from of my Security's gave it as their opinion & advice that I should procd. immediately to Congress to assert my Innocence, and in order that they might have no Plea against me advised and requested me to endeavour to be back by the time the Court sat in Georgia to take my trial there also in case the Congress did not acquit me—which advice I took and set off immediately with Mr. Andrew Donaldson who was going to Philadelphia on the 19th. July without waiting to Send for my Cloathes which was 50 mile out of Town, Mr. Jonan. Bryan accompanyed us 40 mile from Savannah, Mr. D. & myself then proceeded on our Journey without any interuption through So. & North Carolina untill the 6th. of Augt. we then being within 16 mile of Virginia Capt. Nash of the 3d Georgia Battalion came up with us with three or four others and after riding four or five miles in our Company, informed me that he and Col. Ferrel having come to Charlotte a small Town in N Carolina was inform'd that we had passed along some days before, and that Col. Ferrel gave him orders to pursue me with all Speed as also to press Men & Horses, and when he came up with me to shew no kind of Indulgence but on the Contrary to use me in a very rough and harsh manner. Capt. Nashs reply to him was (as he told me) Sir, in obedience to your orders I will pursue Mr. McIntosh but my treatment to that Gentlen. when I come up with him must be left to me. Capt. Nash then shewed me the order the Govr. had given to Col. Ferrel when first he was appointed to go with me to Congress, and added, "Sir I am sorry that I should be sent upon such a disagreable errand but you know I must obey my Superior officers, however Sir you may be assured [end of manuscript]

"Part of Journal in to the Delaware Country
Octobr '78"[61]
We left Camp No.11, about 12 oClock this Day Marched 3 Miles came to the Fork ——— of Muskingum river and

crossed at the old Tuscara war [Tuscarawas] Town. The fording place was very deep owing the snow we have had for these past five howers our brave little Armey who ever [never?] think any thing to [be] too Difficult for them to surmount, plunged Officers & Men into the Creek sometime up to the ——— ——— ——— waters [end of manuscript]

"Journal of the Siege of Charlestown, 1780"[62]

Journal

Ponpon, Parsonage Saturday the 12th. Feby. 1780.

Heard that between forty & fifty Sail of the Enemys Ships came in yesterday at No. Edisto Inlet, and were Landed in force upon Johns Island. Note, the British fleet arrived off Stonoe Inlet the 9th. Feby. (& alarm fired)

Sunday the 13th. February 1780.

Set off this Day with my Family two waggons Northwardly, crossed ponpond River at Parkers ferry, & Lodged this Night at Mr. J. Mcqueen's planta.

Monday the 14th. Feby.

Heard the Enemy Landed some Light Troops at Stonoe,— that our Light Horse were ordered, & upon their March from Sheldon, (our Infantry Stationed there having passed some days ago)—we crossed over Bacon Bridge & through Dorchester to Mr. Lartezettes at Goose Creek where we were detained this Night & all the next Day & Night. Sent Letter to Genl. Lincoln & recd. an Answer giving leave to fix my Family.

Wednesday the 16th. Feby. 1780.

Met Genl. Huger with his Family at Monks Corner going up the Country—here we heard that Murrays ferry [was] impassable with Carriages which determined me to go higher up Santee River to put up this Night at Mr. Thos. Sabbs.

Thursday 17th. Feby.

Baited at Martins and put up this Night at Nelson's Ferry.

Friday the 18th. Feby.

Crossed the Ferry with much difficulty, and Lodged this Night at Colo. Sumpter's where we were weather bound all the next day and night and very genteely treated.

Sunday the 20th. Feby.
Put up this Night at Capt. Richardson's at the entrance of the high Hills.
Monday the 21st. Feby. 1780
Came to a House upon the high Hills belonging to Morton Wilkinson, Just Evacuated by a Capt. Chisolm, where we stayed till Sunday morning trying to get an empty House in this Neighborhood to no purpose.
Sunday the 27th. Feby.
Set off this Morning for Cambden & put up this Night at one McCormicks a Little Inhospitable House over [blank] Creek.
Monday the 28th. Feby. 1780.
Put up this Night at old payn's House upon Pine tree, or Town Creek in Sight of Cambden where we stayed all the next day & were visited by Messrs. Jo. Kershaw Jo. Habersham E. Telfair &ca.
Tuesday the 29th. Feby. 1780
Moved this Evening to a Little Shop in Cambden which was the only Vacant House Colo. Kershaw could procure for me, & was Lyable to be turned out every Hour, as it was engaged for Genl. Huger's Family if they came that Length.
My old Friend & acquaintance Jo. Kershaw was kind enough to promise he would Supply my Family with provision during my absence, & took the few Slaves I had Left to work with his own, upon Shares Saw here the Governors proclamation of 2d. March &ca.
I Stayed here Settling these Matters, & my Family Untill Wednesday the 8th. March 1780.
Sett off this Morning with Lt. Colo. Hopkins (Just from Virginia) for Charlesto.—crossed the Wateree River at Cambden, & took up the Night at Mrs. McCords, Congree Ferry.
Thursday the 9th. March
Baited at the fine Springs of Utaw, & Lodged the Night at [blank's] Tavern at Manigaults Ferry altho my old friend & Country Man Wm. LeConte lived close by—here I met my Son Lackie going from Charlesto. to see his Mother at Cambden in his way to Augusta, & as the direct Road was not Safe traveling, which he experienced going there from ponpon when he Set off from the day we left it.

Friday the 10th. March.
Baited at Martins, & Lodged at Mr. Thos. Sabbs all Night.

Saturday the 11th. March 1780
Heard Cannon all this Day as we rid along the Road, which made us impatient—that Genl. Moultrie who Commanded the Horse at Bacon Bridge was taken Sick, & Genl. Huger Sent to take that Command in his room;—it consisted of Bland's, Boyler's Polaskys [Pulaski's] & Horrys Corps, with Some Voluntiers—altoge[the]r abot. 250 Horse;—came to Charlestown in the Evening, & put up at Mrs. Minis's, tho' disagreeable upon Accot. of some Brittish Prisoners quartered at her House.—Hogans Brigade arrived in Town 3d. Instant.

Sunday the 12th. March
As I did not find Genl. Lincoln at home last Night I waited upon him this Morning,—found the Enemy had possession of James Island since the latter end of Feby. & were now errecting a work upon Bunkers Hill, behind Fort Johnston.—We saw their Fleet, Transports, Store-ships, Merchant Men &ca in Stonoe River, through Wappoe Cut, from Fergusons House in Trad Street & some Men of War over the Barr.—our Horse skirmished near Ashly Ferry.

Monday the 13th. March
The Enemy burnt Fenwick's House on Wappoo Neck (made a Pest House for the Small pox) & errected a Battery there of four (*six*) heavy Cannon, distance [blank] yds from Town.
I was ordered to take the Command of the So. Caro. Country Militia, (See General orders).

Tuesday 14th. March 1780.
The Enemy errected another Battery of two heavy Cannon So. Side of Ashly River about Herveys above the other, & a Bomb Battery upon a rising ground between the two Gun Batteries,—the latter never played.

Wednesday the 15th. March.
A Colonel's Command kept some time past at Ashley Ferry this Side, were withdrawn this day & marched down to Gibb's, abot. 1½ Miles from our Lines, where we had a Picquett before.—only 25 Men for a Look out Left at the ferry.

Thursday the 16th.

The Light Infantry of Hogans Brigade ordered to relieve the Command at Gibbes's—twelve Sail Shipping seen off of the Barr.

Friday the 17th. March.

My Family, Servants, Horses &ca. were moved yesterday to new quarters, Mr. Lowndes House where Genl. Hogun Lodged, near Ferguson's—& early this Morning went to it myself.—recd. Letter by Capt. Nash from president of Congress—date 15th. Feby.

Saturday the 18th.

The Enemy's Ships off the Barr disapeared being Stormy last Night.

Sunday the 19th.

The Enemy's Ships appeared again off the Barr being fine weather.

Monday the 20th.

This Morning the Enemy's Shipping (Men of War) came over the Barr,—8. from 20. to 50. Gunns.

Tuesday the 21st.

Our Ships—the Providence of 30. the Boston of 32. the Queen of France of 18 & the Ranger of 20 Guns Continental, with the Truit (*Adventure*) the Charlestown Militia are ordered from the right of the Lines to the So. Bay as formerly.—General Hogan takes their place on the Line—Genl. Woodford on his Left &c. & ca.

Sunday the 9th.

The Enemy last Night carryed on their approaches from their Left Redoubt, & threw up a Battery for Ten Cannon against the Angle of our advanced Redoubt or half Moon Battery—and the Redan No. 7—Cannonading as usual & some at their Shipping at Fort Johnson without effect.

Monday the 10th. April.

Sr. Henry Clinton & Admiral Arbuthnot sent in a Flagg Summoning the Garrison & Town to Surrender. (See the Summons No. 1)[63]—to which Genl. Lincoln immediately, & without Consulting any one, Sent them for answer, that his Duty & inclination Led him to hold out to the last extremity.—See his Answer in full, No. 2. this Evening Capt. Jno. Gilbank killed by accident in Bolton's Battery &ca. &ca.

Tuesday the 11th.

The Enemy use double diligence now in Compleating their Works & Mounting their Cannon. whilst we ply them with our Cannon and Mortars as Usual, and they from their Gallies & Battery West side of Ashly River in return.— (Jno. Houstoun went over)

Wednesday the 12th.

The Same as yesterday on both sides, it is said some several flat bottomed Boats were hauled on Land by the Enemy across the Neck from Ashly to Cooper River.—

This Day Genl. Lincoln Sent for the General Officers to his Marque & presented a Letter to them directed to Govr. Rutledge which they all Signed Signifying their Opinion in Support of the Generals (already given) that the Governor & part of the Council at least ought to Leave the Garrison, for many Substantial Reasons.

Thursday the 13th. April 1780.

Between Nine & Ten this Morning The Enemy opened all their Gun & Morter Batterys at once (being the first time they fired upon the Town or our Lines upon the front) & continued a furious Cannonade & Bombarding with little intermissions till Midnight, their Batterys from Wappoo playing upon the Left flank of our Lines & the Town at the same time, & their Gallies from Wappoo Creek during the Night as usual, which we returned Smartly from our Lines, & we presume with good effect.— a Sergt. & private of No. Carolina killed, & some Women & Children in Town, the Houses are much damaged & two were burned down near Genl. Moultrie's, Anson bg. [bourough], by Carcases of which they threw several from Ten Inch Mortars.—their Cannon are chiefly twenty four pounders opposite our Lines & 36 pounders upon Wappoo their Morters from $5\frac{1}{2}$ to 13. (*10*) Inches.

one Embrasure at Redan No. 7 destroyed, & also a twenty Six pounder in the flanking Battery on the right, & an eighteen pounder in the Latter dismounted with some other smaller damage.

All the General Officers were called by Genl. Lincoln to his quarters this Morning where he gave us the *first* Idea of the State of the Garrison, the Men, provisions, Stores Artillery &c in it—the little hopes he had of any succour of

Consequence & the opinion of the Engineers respecting our Fortifications: that they were *only Field* works, or Lines, & could hold out but few days more.—with every information he could obtain of the Numbers & Strength of the Enemy &ca. &ca. [he was compelled to] take up the Idea, & Consider of the Propriety of evacuating the Garrison when without hesitation I gave it as my own opinion that as we were so unfortunate as to suffer ourselves to be penned up in the Town, & cut off from all resources in such Circumstances,—we should not loose an hour longer in attempting to get the Continental Troops at Least out, while we had one side open yet over Cooper River, upon whose safety, the Salvation not only of this State but some other will (*may*) probably depend & which I think all the other Gentn. seemd to acquiesce in.

The General said he only desired now that we should consider maturely of the expediency & practicability of such a Measure by the time he would send for us again & the Cannonade mentioned this Morning from the Enemy beginning broke up the Council abruptly.

Governor Rutledge & part of his Council went over Cooper River abt. 12 o'Clock this Day.

Friday the 14th. April

The Enemy are approaching fast upon the right & keep up an Incessant fire from their small Arms, Cannon, and Morters.

a Sergt. of No. Caro. killed by a Cannon Ball—also two Matrosses of So. Caro. & one of Militia Artillery by two of our Cannon going off while they were Loading them Capt. Hill says our Horse were surprised this Day at Monks Corner —killed [blank] Men & an Officer with [blank] Horses taken

Saturday the 15th April.

The Enemy continue Approaching fast on our right.— our Mortars are ordered to the Right to annoy them.—A continual fire of small Arms Cannon & Mortars from the Enemy

A Battery of two Guns opened by the Enemy at Stiles's place on James Island.—which played constantly on the Town —distance across 82. Chain.—many of the Enemys Boats hauled over the Neck into Town Creek.—two of them mounted with brass Cannon came down the Creek this Morning & fired at the Ranger & Adventure

Sunday the 16th.

Two eighteen pounders,—a quantity of Provisions, & other Valuable Articles were got out of the Wreck of the Vessel near Fort Moultrie.—It is said the Enemy attempted to Land on Hobcaw Neck from two Gun Boats, but were prevented by Colo. Malmedy (*Capt. Theus*).—Cannonading &ca. on both sides all day & Night as usual. the new Church Steeple struck by a 24 lb. Ball from James Island Battery.—pits arm broke off &ca.—Major Hogg with detachment of [blank] Men ordered over this night to Lampriers point.

Monday the 18th. say 17th. April

An Inhabitant of the Town killed, & a Woman wounded in bed together.—the approaches continued to the Right.—The Enemy advanced their Bomb Battery within 800. yds. of our Lines.

Note: Signed a Letter Genl. Lincoln brought to my qrs.

Tuesday the 18th. April.

The Enemy continue Aproaching fast.—and firing from their Cannon Mortars & Small Arms.—We advanced a Small Breast Work nearly fronting the square redoubt for Rifle Men, to annoy the Enemy in their Approaches.—Mr. Ph. Neyle A D C. to Genl. Moultrie killed by a Cannon Ball.—two Men killed by small Arms and three wounded by a Shell.—a Soldier of Colo. Neville had an arm shot off by our own Cannon while he was Sentrie outside the Abbaties.—also two french Men wounded, one lost a Legg & the other an Arm.

a twelve pounder burst in the Horn Work by which two Men were much hurt.—the Enemy do not now throw large shells as they have done, but Showers of small ones from their Mortars & Howitzers, which prove very mischievous, especially on our right where one Man was killed & two wounded of the No. Carolinians.

We hear that our Cavalry under Genl. Huger were surprised near Monks Corner & have been totaly defeated, that we lost between 20. & 30 killed & wounded, among the former Major Vernier of Pulaskis Legion—& 150 Horses about forty of the Virginians got in last Night over Cooper River.

A Large party of the Enemy marched up the Country, crossed Wando River & took post at the Church, Hobcaw

Neck.—General Scott with the Light Infantry crossed over Cooper River, to Lampriers before day this Morning with private orders to secure Wapetaw or advantageous Bridge for the retreat of the army &ca. in order to keep open the Communication if possible, as any fresh provision we got was from that quarter.—Lt. Colonels Webster, Tarleton & Robertson are said to have Commanded the Enemy's party who surprised our Horse the 14th. Inst. & gone over Cooper & Wando Rivers afterwards—they say 700 Infy. & 300 Horse

Wednesday the 19th. April.

The Enemy continued their approaches to our right within 250. Yards of the front of the Square redoubt.—and began an approach from the Left Battery towards our advanced Redoubt or half Moon Battery, & moved some of their Mortars into the Latter.—A Considerable party of them shewed themselves before our post at Lampriers this Morning, but soon retreated upon giving them some Cannon Shot.—our party there was too small to pursue them.—Genl. Scot mounted some Men upon his own, & other Officers Horses to reconnoitre them & get intelligence, & then being sent for sett off for Town to a Council of Warr who (*which*) met this Morning at Genl. Moultries Quarters, having attempted it repeatedly before, at Genl. Lincolns, but as often interrupted so much, that we could come to no determination, or do any business; also to accommodate Colo. Lemoy [Laumoy] who was Sick.—besides the General Officers at this Council, Colo. Lamoy and Colo. Beekman were called to it to represent the Engineer & Artillery Departmts. & Colo. Simmons as Commdt. of the Town Militia when the subject first proposed to be considered upon the 13th Instant, & several times since at our Meetings was again offered by Genl. Lincoln, & the Returns of the Army, Comissarys (*Provisions &ca. &ca.*) laid before the Council with a charge of the greatest Secrecy in that as well as any determination that may be taken. Some Gentlemen seem'd still inclined to an evacuation notwithstanding the difficulty appeared much greater now than when formerly (*first*) Mentioned, which was my own opinion, also, & I proposed Leaving the Militia for the Guards &ca. in Garrison.— untill the Continental Troops Cleared themselves but was carryed against us by the arguments of

Colo. Lemoy and for offering Honl. terms of Capitulation upon Hon. Terms fixed—in the Midst of our Conference the Lt. Governor Gadsden happened to come in whether by Accident or design is not known, & General Lincoln proposed he might be allowed to Sit as one of the Council, he appeared surprised & displeased that we had entertained a thought of a Capitulation or evacuating the Garrison, and (*tho he*) acknowledged himself entirely ignorant of the State of the provisions &ca. &ca. before, but said he would Consult his Council & promised that if it was determined by us to Capitulate, he would Send such Articles as they required for the Citizens of Charlestown in an hour or two.

Adjourned in the Evening to Genl. Lincolns quarters where Colo. Lamoy representing the insufficienty of our Fortifications (if they were worthy of being called so) the improbability of holding out many days Longer, & the impracticability of making our Retreat good as the Enemy were now situated, carryed it for offering (*trying first*) terms of Honle. Capitulation first Unanimously in whieh I Joined after requesting to be the last Voiee, as all the rest had been of that opinion. The Lt. Govr. with four of his Council Messrs. Ferguson Hutson Cattle & Dr. Ramsey in a Little after, Used the Council very Rudely, the Lt. Govr. declaring he would protest against our proceedings.—that the Militia were willing to Live upon Rice alone rather than give up the Town upon any Terms.—& that even the old Women were so accustomed to the Enemys Shot now that they traveled the Streets without fear or dread, but if we were determined to Capitulate he had his terms in his pocket ready. Mr. Ferguson on the other hand said [illegible word] the Inhabitants of the Town observed several days (*some time*) ago the Boats Collected together to carry off the Continental Troops, but that they would keep a good Watch upon us the army & if it was ever attempted he would be among the first who would open the Gates for the Enemy and assist them in attacking us before we got aboard.

After the Lt. Govr. & Counselors were gone some time, Colo. C. C. Pinkney came in abruptly upon the Council, & forgetting his usual Politeness, addressed Genl. Lincoln in great warmth & much the same Strain as the Lt. Governor had done, adding that those who were for business required no Councils & that he came over on purpose from Fort Moultrie to prevent any terms being offered the Enemy or evacuating the Garrison, & addressing himself to Colo. Lemoy, charged the Engineer Dept. with being the sole Authors & promoters of any proposals &ca. &ca.

I was myself so much hurt by the repeated Insults given to the Commanding Officer in so public a Manner, & obliquely to us all through him, that I could not help declaring as it was thought impracticable to get the Continental Troops out I was for holding the Garrison to the last extremity, which was at once agreed to except by Colo. Lamoy who said we were already come to the last extremity, or if we were not of that opinion, desired, to know what we called the last extremity. but it was carryed without other opposition to hold out & we parted this Night.—I desired a Letter Signed by Genl. Moultrie & myself the 17th. might be destroyed which [was] done before us.

Thursday 20th. June [sic] 1780.

This morning fourteen Sail of Shipping appeared off of the Barr said to be a Reinforcement to General Clinton, having a fine day, cold & windy.—two of our Magazines blown up by shells in Gibs Battery on the right; only one man hurt, but much other damage

This day General Lincoln called a Council of Warr again, same Members as yesterday.—and the same Subjects debated on.—Colo. Lamoy still insisting upon the Impossibility of holding out the Garrison much Longer, and a Retreat seeming to him impracticable, proposed, that the Honle. Terms of Capitulation should first be offered, which possibly might be accepted by Genl. Clinton, or, if it did not succeed that we might then attempt a retreat if we thought it could be accomplished.

The opposition now expected from the Citizens of the Town in evacuating it, in addition to the former obstacles we had in consideration Vizt. a Large party of Foot & Horse upon Wando Neck, & a number of the Enemys boats hawled aCross Charlesto. Neck from Ashly into Cooper River &ca. induced the whole Council to come into the Cornels [Colonels] proposal and make the Tryal. I requested to be the last in giving our Votes.—Upon which we parted.

The Enemys approach continues on our left,—their Mortars moved from the left battery into their approaches.—an 18 pounder dismounted in Capt. Ballards Battery on our right.—four of the Enemy's Gallies that Lay in Wappoo Creek, & came in to Ashly River about every night since 4th. Insta. went down abot. Nine o'Clock this night to their Shipping at Fort Johnston, under a very heavy firing from all our batterys West & So. of the Town.—The Enemy Retreated from Hobcraw across Wappetaw Bridge &ca.

Friday the 21st. 1780. April.

A Flagg sent from us to Genl. Clinton, requiring a Truce for Six Hours, to consider upon Terms of Capitulation (See No. 3)[64] which is granted (See No. 4). & afterwards prolonged by Messenger.—The Articles proposed & Sent by Genl. Lincoln were made out by himself and Colo. Ternant, without his General Officers (See No. 5)—but they were called in the Evening to Genl. Lincoln's Tent, to consider upon Genl. Clinton & Adml. Arbuthnot's Reply No. 6 which after some hours spent in finding Copy of the Articles we sent out, was unanimously agreed to be a Rejection of the whole, & that a Messenger should be sent out to inform them they might begin firing again when they pleased—which they did immediately abot. Nine at night with greater Virilence & fury than ever, & continued it without intermission till day Light & was returned smartly from the Garrison.

The Enemy open'd two Embrasures against our battery No.4—a twelve pounder dismounted in Redan No.7. the killed & wounded lately are so many they cannot be ascertained.—Colo. Tinning of No. Carol: with his Regmt. of Militia abot. 200 came over from Lampriers, & Joined my Brigade.

Saturday the 22d. April.

Our Ration this day order'd to be reduced to 3/4 lb. of Beef.—Lt. Colo. Laurens with his Lt. Infantry to return from Lampriers to Town & resume his former post—see orders.

The Enemy kept up a heavy Cannonade, & approach fast on our left in front of the advanced Redoubt or half Moon battery.—three men wounded &ca.—they made several Boyaux from their second parralell.

The 23rd. April. Sunday

The Enemys approaches continualy carrying on upon

our Right & Left, those on our Right within 20. yds of our dam.—a Mortar moved from the right of Colo. Parkers Encampment.—abot. eight at Night two Deserters from the Enemy.—they confirm the report of a considerable Reinforcement from New York.—that they detached Ten Companys of Light Infantry to go over to Hadrells point.—and say the Enemy lost a Number of Men lately by our Shells.

Monday the 24th.

A party of 200 Men detached from the Virginians & So. Caro: Lines under the Command of Lt. Colo. Henderson Sallyed out at day Light this Morng. opposite the half Moon or advanced Battery, upon the Enemy's approaches & compleatly Surprised them, in their trenches abot. fifteen of them were killed with the Bayonet in their ditches, & twelve Prisoners brought off.—Seven of whom were wounded. —the Enemy attempted to Support them, but were obliged to retreat upon our giving them some rounds of Grape Shot, the prisoners say Major Hall of the 74th. Regt. Commanded them but no Officer was to be found.—Capt. Moultrie killed, & two privates wounded upon our side in our Retreat.—the whole was done in a few Minutes without our partys firing a Single Gun, & in the greatest order.

It is said Colo. C. C. Pinckney & Lt. Colo. Laurens assured Gen. Lincoln they could (keep the pass of Lampriers open, and) Supply the Garrison with plenty of Beef from Lampriers point upon which the Commissary was ordered to Issue a full allowance again as before the order of 22d. (See orderly B[ook?]) but unfortunately the first, & only Cattle Butchered at Lampriers for the use of the Garrison were altogether Spoiled & useless through Neglect or Mismanagement before they came over.—these Gentlemen are said also to have some days past promised to keep the Communication open on the Cooper River Side, & besides Beef, to send a sufficient Number of Negroes over to Town for the works which were much wanted.—(Kelly's).

Lt. Colo. Laurens with the Lt. Infantry, & Colo. C. C. Pinckney with the greater part (or almost the whole) of the 1st So. Caro. Regt. came into Garrison this Morning from Lampriers, & ordered into the Horn Work & to Mount the Port Guard.—Major Harris & 75 of his Regt. No. Caro:

Militia ordered to Lampriers under the direction of Colo. Malmady, who with Major Hogg is left to Command that post.–& Lt. Colo. Scott with [blank] of the 1st. So. Caro Regm. & abot. [blank] Militia to Command at Fort Moultrie.

Colo. Parker of the Virginians killed abot. eight this Evening by a Rifle Ball looking over the Parapet of the half Moon battery.–two privates killed also & Seven wounded, with several others not known having kept an incessant Fire of Cannon, Mortars & small Arms on both Sides.

Tuesday the 25th. April.

Between twelve & one this Morning a heavy fire of Cannon & Musketry, from our advanced redoubts & the right of our Lines, occasioned (it is said) by the Enemy's advancing in Collumn.–it is certain they gave several Huzzas, & abused us, calling us bloody Doggs, being upon duty myself & upon the Lines all the Night; but whether they were out of their trenches is not so clear.–it was forty or fifty Minutes before I could put a Stop to the waste of Ammunition untill we could make sure of a proper object.–the Enemy returned the fire Smartly & threw several Light balls & Carcasses into Town.

about two oClock this Afternoon Lord Cornwallis with about 3000 Men took possession of Mount Pleasant, Hadrils Pt. abot. 2 oClock P.M. having crossed from Chs. Town Neck over Cooper River to [blank] last Night. (three men wounded J. H. [John Habersham]).

Wednesday the 26th.

The small Ship Lord George Germaine & a Sloop Joined the Enemy's fleet near Fort Johnston after passing Fort Moultrie at a great distance with little or no damage.–some of the Enemy's Ships remain'd below in five fathom hole.–& it was said two of 74. Guns Lay off the Barr.–the Vigilant Capt. Brett at Beaufort.–The Enemy pretty quiet Yesterday and last Night: we suppose they are bringing Cannon into their third Paralel.–they are seen Strengthening their approaches.– and in Possession of Mount Pleasant.

Brigr. Genl. DuPortail arrived from Philadelphia which he left the 3d Insta.–where he says there was no Prospect of our getting any Reinforcement soon from our grand Army.– Congress having only proposed to G. Washington (then at Morristown) the Sending the Maryland Line.

One Man killed,—Capt. Goodwin of 3d. So. Carolina and one private wounded. (J. H.) [John Habersham] (De Bra:) [Ferdinand de Brahm] the Enemy began their third parralel.

Thursday the 27th.
Last Night Colo. Malmady with his Detachmt. at Lampriers ferry retreated in great confusion across the River, after Spiking up four 18 pounders they left behind.—about one in afternoon four of the Enemy Gallies, and Armed Sloop, & a frigate moved down the River, and Anchor'd opposite, & near the Mouth of Hogg Island, after a very faint opposition from the Cannon of Fort Moultrie.—one of the Galleys got aground & was lost.

5 Militia Men of James Isld. (Capt. Stiles's) deserted last Night in a boat.—(J. H.) one private killed & five wounded.

Tarr Bbs. ordered to be fixed before our Lines every Evening, & burn all Night to prevent a Surprise, as the Enemy are close to the Cannal, & keep up almost a continued runing fire of small Arms Night & Day upon us.—A pickett of a Field Officer & 100 Men of my Militia Brigade ordered every evening to Gadsdens old House, to Support a small Guard of a Sergt. & 12 Regulars upon the Wharf in case of an attack by the Enemy Boats upon that quarter.—Major Pinckney ordered out on some duty.

Friday the 28th.
Two Deserters from the Enemy at Hobcaw brought over by our Troops.—we See the British flagg flying at our late post Lampriers.—Major Low and Several Supernumery Officers quitted the Garrison over Cooper River.

The Enemy very busy throwing up their third Paralel, within a few yards of our Canal, which in most places is above 100 yards from our breast work.

Our fatigue hard at work enclosing the Horn Work.—the few Negroes remaining in Town are obliged to be pressed daily, & kept under guard, as the masters as well as the Slaves, were unwilling they should work. (J. H.) two privates killed. Lt. Campaign of No. Carolina & two privates wounded.

Saturday the 29th.
The Enemys third Paralel nearly finished, and a Redoubt begun toward the Middle of it. (De Bra:) opposite the Gate & another towards our left (J. H.)

Our hands began a retired Redoubt on the right of the horn work.—General Lincoln informed the General Officers privately that he intended the Horn Work as place of retreat for the whole Army in Case they were drove from the Lines.—I observed to him the impossibility of those who were Station'd at the So. Bay & Ashly River retreating there in Such Case, to which he replyed that we might Secure ourselves as best we could.

A Heavy Bombardment from the Enemy during the Night.—& small Arms never ceasing.—

A Deserter from them, Says, they are preparing a bridge to throw over the Canal.

Capt. Templeton of the 4th Geo. Regt. wounded by Shell.

Tattoo ordered not to beat.

Colo. Malmady ordered to deliver a written report of the Evacuation of Hobcaw, &ca. &ca.

Sunday April the 30th:

General Lincoln received a Letter from Govr. Rutledge upon which he Congratulates the Army in Genl. orders for hearing of a Large Reinforcement that may open our Communication again to the Country, &ca.

The Deserters Yesterday tell us; the Huzzas which Occasioned the firing last Tuesday Morning were from the Enemy's working party, who thought we were Sallying.— the Engineers he Says ordered them when that happened to give three Cheers, & fall back upon their Covering party.— who not having been apprised of it, received them as an Enemy, in consequence of which a considerable Number of them were killed & Wounded.—he confirms the Account of their receiving a considerable reinforcement from New York, & says the last Detachmt. sent to Hobcaw Amounts to above two thousand, that they expect their Shipping up to Town every Night,—& are preparing a Large Number of faschines to fill up the Cannal.

Severe firing of Cannon, Mortars & Small Arms continued on both Sides.—Lt. Campen & Ensign Hall of No. Caro: wounded badly, & Lt. Philips of the Virginians.—privates killed & wounded not known there are so many.

I think it is this day that Genl. Lincoln called the Genl. Officers together at his Quarters, that Genl. duportail who had viewed our fortifications might give us his opinion respecting them, and the State of the Siege, which was in Substance much the Same as Colo. Lamoy repeatedly expressed before Vizt. that our works could only be called field Lines, & could hold out but very few Days &ca. &ca.—He brought the printed Resolve of Congress respecting me,—which was laid before Council.

Monday the 1st. May 1780.

Our Fatigue imployed errecting another Redoubt on the left of the horn work, & compleating these new works intended for a retreat in Case of Necessity.

The Enemy appear to be about another Battery in their third paralel, opposite No.12 on our right.—five men deserted last Night, from the Gallie which yet remained in Wappoo Creek.—the many risques they run in the attempt is astonishing.—A very Smart Bombardmt. kept up during this day.

Capt. Mumford of No. Caro: wounded by a Muskt. ball.— and Mr. P. Lord a Voluntier killed yesterday by a Shell.

Tuesday the 2d. May.

Last Night the Enemy made a ditch on the right to drain our Cannal.

A Number of Men killed & wounded the last three or four days, which cannot be ascertained.

A General Monthly Return ordered to be made, with Accot. of the killed wounded & Deserted since 1st. Aprl:

A nine pounder burst in battery No. 12,—and a quantity of fixed Ammunition blown up by accident in batterys No. 10 & 12.

It is said the Enemy throw Shells at us Charged with Rice & Sugar.

Lt. Colo. Smith of Town Militia with a party to press Negroes for the works—if possible.

Wednesday the 3d.

Cannonading, Bombarding & continual firing wth. small Arms as Usual on both Sides.

Our fatigue imployed fetching Picketts &ca.

Thursday the 4th.

Lt. Gerrard wounded.

Our Rations reduced to 6 oz. of Meat, & bad enough.— Coffee & Sugar allowed the Soldiers with their Rice.

the Enemy appear to have possession of our battery on the

end of Gadsden's Bridge Leading to Fort Moultrie. Fire from the Enemy's Cannon Slack but they do not spare shells & small Arms.—our Hospital Ship carryed away.

From Colo. Bernard Beekman's Notes.[65]
On or Abot. the 12th. February 1780, Gen. Lincoln called Br. Genl. Moultrie, and Colonels C. C. Pinckney, Heath, Lamoy, Malmady, Beekman, to a Council at his quarters;—informed them the British Troops Landed in different parts of this State to the So. ward, & were said to be marching to Charlestown.—laid several Returns before them, giving the Number of Continl. Troops now in the State, the Number he expected, & the Prospect he had of being Joined by the Militia of this State & No. Carolina.—the General also informed the Council he had ordered Colo. Parker with his Command down from Augusta, and then put this Question.

Do you think it expedient that all, or any part of our Army go out to Meet the Enemy, & attack them, as we may have opportunity on their March to Town?

Answered in the Negative, by all, but Colo. Malmady.

It was then Resolved, that all the Continental Troops should be immediately called to Charlestown, & its vicinage except the Horse & two Light Companys of Foot, who were to Harrass the Enemy on their March as occasion offered.

15th. Feby. 1780.

A Majors Command, with a party of the Charlesto. Artillery & one field Piece, ordered to take post near Ashley Ferry.

24th. Feby.

The Command near Ashley ferry reinforced to a Lt. Colo. 4 Captains, 4 Subs. 8 Sergts. 8 Corps. & 150 privates;— the Artillery as before Vizt: 1 Sergt. & 7 Men.

Genl. Lillington of No. Carolina with his Militia came to Charlesto. about this time.

Collo. Lytle says, he came himself with two of the No. Caro: Militia Regts. abot. a fortnight before Genl. Lillington, and the General brought the two other Regiments.—made 4 in all.

The 9th. of March 1780.

Captains Mathews, Wilson & Mitchels Companys of Militia ordered to Fort Moultrie.

"From Major H[abersha]m's Journal of the Siege."
He begins the 28th. March 1780, & Says—
This Day the Enemy crossed Ashley River in force above the Ferry.

Wednesday the 29th. March.
The Enemy advanced on the Neck.—the Light Infantry were this Evening reinforced with two Companys, & the Command of the whole given to Lt. Colo. Laurens.

Thursday the 30th. March.
The Enemy came on as far as Gibbes's, where they continued Skirmishing throughout the Day with our Lt. Infantry, who were reinforced in the Evening with two field pieces & Ninety Men.
Our party retired into Garrison abot. dark.—killed Capt. Bowman of No. Carolina—wounded Major Hyrne & seven privates.—The Enemy were all this day transporting Troops from old posts on Wappoo Neck to Gibbes's.

Friday the [31st March.]
The Garrison [busily employed throwing up works.—Mounting Cannon etc. all Day].

Satu[rday the 1st April.]
Our Troops [employed as yesterday]

Sunday the 2d. April 1780.
Last Night the Enemy broke ground, and this morning appeared two Redoubts.—one nearly opposite our Nine Gun Battery, on the right of the Horne Work, & another a little to the Left of the Same at about 1200. Yards distance from our Lines.

Monday the 3d.
The Enemy employed in compleating their two Redoubts, and errecting another on the Left, nearly opposite Battery No. 4.—at about an equal distance with the rest.

Tuesday the 4th.
Several Deserters within the past three or four days, who say the Enemy, on Thursday last, had upwards of twenty Men killed and wounded: among the Latter was a Lt. Colonel of the 60th. Regt.—Lord St. Clair badly: & that they are bringing their heavy Cannon on the Neck. Since the appearance of the Enemy's Works, they have been Cannonaded. —two Ten Inch, and [one Seven Inch] Mortars were removed from the [Bay to play upon them].

Wednesday the 5th. April 1780.

Last Night the Enemy continued their Approaches to Hamstead Hill, on which they errected a Battery for twelve Cannon, & a Mortar battery a Little in the Rear.—The Cannon & Mortars of the Garrison employed as usual in annoying their Works.—the Batterys on Wappoo Neck & the Gallies Cannonaded the Town all last night.—by which one of the Inhabitants was Killed in Kingstreet, and two Horses at Genl. McIntosh's quarters.

Thursday the 6th.

The Enemy approached from their centre Redoubt & errected a five Gun battery, on the Angle between Batterys No. 11 & 12.—The Virginians under Brigr. General Woodford got in by the way of Addison's ferry, & some Militia of No. Carolina under Colo. Harrington.

Friday the 7th.

This afternoon twelve sail of the Enemys Shipping passed Fort Moultrie, under a very heavy Cannonade: one of them supposed to be a Store Ship, having met with some accident ran aground in the Cove, where she was blown up by her own people. The remainder consisting of one fifty, and two forty four gun Ships, four frigates, two Ships supposed to be Transports a Schooner & a Sloop, Anchored under Fort Johnston.

Saturday the 8th.

The Enemy employed in finishing their Batterys on our right.

Sunday the 9th.

The Enemy Last night continued their approaches from their Redoubt on our Left, and threw up a battery for Ten Cannon against the Angle of our advanced redoubt, and the Redan No.7.— Some Shot were throw'n at the Shipping by our Batterys on the Bay, without effect.

Monday the 10th. April.

Sr. Henry Clinton & Admiral Arbuthnot summon'd the Town to surrender, in the following terms Vizt.

Here follows the Summons [omitted].—and General Lincoln's Answer to it [omitted]. Verbatim, to which be reffered.

Tuesday & Wednesday the 11th & 12th.

The Enemy busy in compleating their Works, and [mounting their Cannon].

JOURNALS 115

Thursday the 13th. April 1780.

Between Nine & Ten this Morning, the Enemy opened all their Gun & Mortar Batterys, and continued a furious Cannonade & Bombardment with short intermissions untill Midnight the Gallies & Batterys on Wappoo Neck firing also.—One Embrasure at Redan No.7 destroyed, a Sergt. & private of No. Carolina killed.—a twenty six pounder destroy'd and an eighteen pounder dismounted in the flanking battery on the right.—some Women and Children killed in Town.—The Enemys Cannon are chiefly twenty four pounders, and their Mortars from 5 1/2. to 10. Inches.

They threw Carcasses from Ten Inch Mortars by which two Houses near Genl. Moultrie's were burned.

Friday the 14th. &ca. &ca.

[End of McIntosh's copy of Major Habersham's Journal].

- - - - - - - - - -

Subaltern's Journal.

[First six pages are so badly mutilitated they are illegible].

20th [April]

The enemy [words torn off] by Capt. Alex. [words torn off] few men woun[ded] [words torn off] Generals and [words torn off] horses—who rep[ort] that they were at the distance of eighteen Miles from the post near Wappetaw bridge, which they had cut down, & Seem'd preprar'd for marching." that they had cut down many trees in the road to prevent a pursuit.

The General early this day sent for the attend [words torn off] Charlestown. [Remainder of entry mutilated].

21st.

A Cessation of hostilities this day—flags passing to and from the enemy. The subject not known by us subalterns but Strongly suspected to be terms, for a Capitulation.

The Parties that had been sent from the post at Lampriers [words torn off] few negroes [words torn off] hundred Cattle [words torn off].

At a [words torn off]—putation it was allow'd that thirty Cattle per day Would afford the Garrison of Charlestown at least half allowance of fresh beef the other half to be Serv'd in Salt provision.

Colo. Malmady who commanded at the posts, the General being in town at Council order'd the whole to be slaughter'd and sent to town. By the negligence [words torn off] [pe]ople who [words torn off] to super–[words torn off] Commissaries & [words torn off] the whole were render'd useless. They being so utterly Spoil'd when they arriv'd at the Garrison, as not to be eat.

The Occasion of the truce this day was an Offer to the enemy of the town upon honorable terms. The General Officers being acquainted that the Magazines of provisions were nearly exhausted. The terms f[or capitulation] were rejected [words torn off] And none ot[her were] Offered by us. [Hos]tilities Commenc'd this night, an incessant fire being kept up on each side.

Our prospect of success in the defence entirely depended on the hopes of part of the Northern Army and Militia falling on the enemies rear and obliging them to raise the siege. And our own perseverance which was flatter'd by the Commandant [words torn off] and that [words torn off] Infantry. They [words torn off] effectually to keep open the communication between the town and Country, and to supply the Garrison with fresh provision, and Negroes to assist at the additions to be made to our imperfect fortifications.

It will be necessary in this place to take some notice of the behaviour of the generality of the inhabitants [words torn off] part of the [words torn off] was some shew [words torn off] them of turning out Militia to guard small posts and landings which might be attempted by the Enemy. The appearance of performing this service was preserved while no real danger was apprehended, and they had an opportunity of living well at the expence of the Country.

When the Enemy approached [words torn off] duty, openly [words torn off] Officers. They had no no[tion] of running the risque of being taken in Arms, and that it was much more safe and prudent to meet them at their own houses where they would procure protections from the Commanding Officer, Lt. Col. Webster.

This loyal resolution they literally executed & Supplied the enemy with every thing they could afford, and piloted [words torn off] places as the [words torn off] were occupied [words torn off] small parties which they intended to surprise.

Such of the Militia Officers as had more Virtue than the privates returned to the post at Lamprie's recounting this shameful revolt.

Had this happen'd in any other State the Offenders might possibly have been brought to punishment & obedience—but the General [words torn off] which prevaild [words torn off] where, prevented it. The Weakness of our Garrison, and the Strength of the enemy's force which lay before it render'd us unable to be Masters of the adjacent Country and oblig'd us to keep close within our own Works.

22d of [April]

Sent for by [words torn off] come to town w[ith our] baggage.

Arriv'd in the evening Heavy firing from both Sides. The approaches towards our Works carried on briskly by the enemy. Much execution done by their Shells—which were thrown upon every part of our lines. The Number Wounded and Kill'd difficult to be ascertain'd. From the 21st it was allow'd there were fifteen lost each day from the Continentals [words torn off] known which happened [words torn off] the Militia, who were posted on the bay and only expos'd to the fire of the shipping.

Alarm this night. the enemy approaching to our gate & appearing in Column as if intending a Storm.

An heavy Cannonade from our lines. The Soldiers on the right beginning to fire, it ran through the ranks and for a few minutes one continued roar from the Cannon & Small Arms.

The Enemy [words torn off] fire ceas'd.

Sergeant Lej—[torn off] of Parkers kill'd by a shell this day.

24th.

At day break Lt. Colo. Henderson, Majr. Stephenson & two hundred men from Genl. Woodfords & Scotts Brigades made a Sortie on the Enemy in the trenches. The assault was conducted with Conduct & Success. Our Men attacked with the Bayonet killd about twenty wounded near as many, and took twelve Prisoners.

The Enemy were discovered this night working near our half moon Battery. Col. Richard Parker having reconoitred them return'd to the Battery to direct the fire. When the Yagres sending a platoon of rifles into the Embrasure [words torn off] shot the Colo. through [words torn off] he died immediately [H]is Character is so well known, it need not to be said, how much he is regretted.

Capt. Moultrie killd at the Sortie.

Lampries ferry evacuated by Col. Malmady—retreat disorderly. lost Lieut. Worsham of Russells regimt. and twenty privates of the Virginia line, who were left as a party to cover the embarkation of the rest. He and the party taken Coming down the River.

Pinkney's Regt. which were Stationed at Fort Moultrie call'd to the Garrison. Three Companies of [blank] being left to defend that post with some Militia.

25th [April]

The Approaches of [words torn off] heavy Cannonading [words torn off] till the Sixth of May, much mischief done daily by the Shells. Lieut. Phillips of Col. Russels regiment killd in the half moon by a shell Mr Peter Lord of the Militia killd at the same time. Circumstances begin now to grow some what alarming—from the allowance of provision being Curtaild, strict search made in the Houses of the Inhabitants for this article some discovered; but inadequate to the supplies necessary. Soldiers notwithstanding the many inconveniences and fatigue they Suffered are in high Spirits.

Capt. Templeton of the Artilery died of the wound he received from a Shell.

5th [May]

Fort Moultrie surrendered to the British Forces—this fort by many people was reckoned impregnable yet the want of provision and the weakness of the Garrison obliged it to surrender, greatest of the regt. which was posted there being ordered to reinforce the Town.

Lt Colo. Scott of South Carolina commanded the fort at the Surrender. terms &ca.

This affair damp'd the Spirits of the Citizens, tho not of the Army. All communication between the City and Country were now cut off and the Garrison and Citizens entirely dependant on there own Stores which were exhausted to a few days shot allowance Some days before this accident Colo. Malmady having no command and being somewhat disagreable to the Garrison in Consequence of the affair at Lampriers was advised to quit the town while there was a probability of a passage.

He set out in a boat accompanied by Edward Rutledge Esqr. late a member of Congress & who had served till this time of the seige with reputation as Captain in Charles Town Artilery there were also two men of suspected Characters.

They were taken by the Enemy upon landing Malmady attempted to escape; meeting with a Negro he desired him to pilot him clear of the British Camp.

The negro intending to do the enemy a favor conducted him close to their lines which Malmady perceiving drew on him and cut him several times. The Negroe closed with him and drawing a knife wounded him so [severely] we hear he is since died. The average of the killed each day amounted to fifteen by shells, shot &ca.

6th [May]

This day Sir Henry Clinton sent proposals of surrender to us begining with a preamble that it proceeded from his humanity and desire to spare the effusion of human blood Counsel of Genl. and field officers call'd. Governor and Council also to be consulted.

7th [May]

Negociations continued—Various conjectures concerning the acception or rejection of our proposals

8th [May]

Truce continued till 8 oClock in the evening. our proposals were rejected and hostilities commenced at the time above mentioned

Although it was [words torn off] subsistence of the Garrison must depend entirely upon what rice was conceald in Town by the Inhabitants for private [use] and this quantity known to be but small.

Yet some persons were clear for opposition, and insisted upon such Terms as they were certain would not be complied with, yet ignorant of the most distant means of Succour or resource.

These people consisting chiefly of those who were possessed of property in the Town joind only by two Continental land and one Naval officer outweighed the Counsil—and renew'd the fire.

The Cannonade opened with three Cheers on each side and continued without intermission the whole night.

[9th May]

Hostilities continued, orders for the purchasing Commissary to seize every steer and cow in the town for the use of the Garrison—Warm fire from the Enemy this day—there approaches are now so near as to do certain execution with their Musquetry above twenty men killed this day. Soldiers more active than the Commissary, drive the Cattle into the range of the Shells where some are kill'd which they soon divide an agreable repast after some days want of meat since the approaches of the enemy became so alarming. Tarr barrels were light every night near the Abbatis in order to discover there advances should they attempt to Storm. Ensign [name missing] one of those receiving a wound through the body of which he died next day. Whispered this night that the Inhabitants of the Town (Militia) were framing a petition to Genl. Lincoln begging of him to accept the terms offer'd by Genl. Clinton—at the same time many of them refusing to do further duty.

The Allowance of Provision consisted now of a little Coffee sugar and rice.

10th

Militia abandon the lines and cannot be prevail'd upon to Join. Cannon entirely deserted two pieces in the half moon dismounted and one unfit for use. This Battery unable to make [words missing] circumstances alarming. Capt. Valentine Peyton firing a Cannon which was deserted and in front of which the enemy were working uncovered Shot through the Head—died almost immediately much lamented. Adjutant Ferrell killd by a shell. at four oClock this afternoon a flag was sent from us to desire a negociation with the enemy. The Militia were now convinced they were deceived in their conjectures of the Quantity of provision and other Stores and sincerely desired the acceptation of Terms

11th

Negociations continued the Soldiers not served with provision. people of the Town flock to the Lines. The Butcher who destroyed the meat at Lampriers being somewhat insolent at Hopkin's Regiment was very roughly handled.

Hungry guts in the Garrison.

12th

Capitulation agreed on. Detachment of Grenadiers takes possession of the Horn Work at three o'Clock our troops march out and pile there Arms, they return and are dismissed to their Tents. The enemies Guard take possession of the Town.

13th

At twelve this day ordered from the Lines—the Officers to empty houses and the Soldiers to the Barracks.

By the [terms] of Capitulation we understand that the Officers were to wear their Swords, yet the enemy affirm that although it was allowed us to retain, yet we should not wear them—and insist that this was the true Spirit of the Article. we were obliged to lay them down—that is, keep them out of sight. no provision this day.

14th

This day pass'd disagreeably—ordered to attend for paroles at different times, when there always was something to prevent there being fill'd. Officers and men of the Continental line ordered to parade at the Barracks at twelve this day to be reviewed by Genl. Leslie or an Officer appointed by him the above order postponed untill Tomorrow Morning.

15th

Troops paraded according to order this day. Genl. Leslie attended. The Enemy very much surprised at the smallness of our Numbers. While the men were on the parade at the Barracks the Arsenal where we used to keep our fixed Ammunition where our Arms and the pistols & Swords of the Militia were deposited this day by the enemy was blown up accidently—as near as we can learn two hundred lives were lost—one half the enemies Guard and Artilery with three officers—the other Inhabitants who resided near. the Lunaticks and negroes who were chained in Goal for trifling Misdemeanours. Some un[thin]king men of the enemy imagined it was perpertrated by our party but the more Sensible are certain it was occasioned by the firing of one of the Guns which they were laying in the Store as most of our Soldiers Guns when delivered were loaded—and one had fir'd in the same place Yesterday by being so roughly handled in a removal.

Contiguous to the Arsenal there was a Magazine which contained thirty thousand wt. of Powder which it was expected would take fire. The Inhabitants were much alarmed and both they and the British who were quartered at the end of the Town removed their effects—during this Confusion which this fire Occasioned both [words missing] who were on parade were Strongly guarded by a detachment of Hessians. however when the danger abated & peace was restored Genl. Leslie returnd, made some apology for our Detention from our quarters & we as prisoners were glad to be released.

During the confusion the british much alarm'd, Patrolls in the Streets till the fire was extinguish'd their whole Garrison under Arms.

16th

Genl. field Commissioned & other officers ordered to attend for their paroles, but put off till Tomorrow

Officers almost tir[e]d with attendance.

[End of Journal]

Notes

Introduction

1. William MacKenzie to William B. Hodgson, Sept. 28, 1844, and Nov. 1, 1844, in William MacKenzie Papers, Georgia Historical Society.
2. The two names for the settlement have been misused in several accounts. Bessie Lewis in her "Darien, a Symbol of Defiance and Achievement," *Georgia Historical Quarterly*, XX (Sept. 1936), 185-198 (hereafter cited as *G.H.Q.*), established beyond doubt the correct sequence of their usage.
3. John McIntosh Mor is often referred to as John Moore McIntosh. Mor (Moor, Mohr) was not a middle name; it signified "large" and was used to distinguish him from others of the same name, some of whom came to Georgia with him. He invariably signed his name John McIntosh M. *Columbian Museum and Savannah Advertiser*, Dec. 13, 1796, p. 3, col. 3; "Genealogy of the Georgia Branch of the McIntosh Family," by Alexander Mackintosh, which was compiled for the Georgia Historical Society in 1844 and sent to the Society by William MacKenzie. It is now in the Keith Read Collection, The University of Georgia Library.
4. A. D. Candler, ed., *Colonial Records of the State of Georgia*, IV (Atlanta, 1906), 165. We ascertain that Lewis was the unfortunate victim, for Phineas was reported "Alive at Darien, 1741."
5. The quotations, the list of the family which came to Georgia, and other genealogical data are from E. M. Coulter and A. B. Saye, eds., *A List of the Early Settlers of Georgia* (Athens, 1949); *Georgia Gazette*, Feb. 11, 1796, p. 2, col. 2; J. G. B. Bulloch, *A History and Genealogy of the Family of Baillie of Dunain . . . With a Short Sketch of the Family of McIntosh, Bulloch and Other Families* (Green Bay, Wis., 1898), 68-73, 83-86; William MacKenzie to William B. Hodgson, Sept. 28, 1844; McIntosh Genealogy by Alexander Mackintosh, cited above. There is so much confusion in accounts of the McIntosh family due to identical names in different branches and generations that the editor felt it necessary to include details of Lachlan McIntosh's family.
6. *Columbian Museum and Savannah Advertiser*, Feb. 24, 1801, p. 3, col. 1.
7. *Ibid.*, Dec. 13, 1796, p. 3, col. 3.
8. *Collections of the Georgia Historical Society*, XII (Savannah, 1957), 99 (hereafter cited as *Colls. G.H.S.*).
9. *National Portrait Gallery of Distinguished Americans* (Philadelphia, 1836); George White, *Historical Collections of Georgia* (New York, 1854), 334-335; Sarah B. G. Temple and Kenneth Coleman, *Georgia Journeys* (Athens, 1961), 231.
10. *National Portrait Gallery of Distinguished Americans* (Philadelphia, 1836).
11. For an account of McIntosh's career in the Western Department see "A Revolutionary Journal and Orderly Book of General Lachlan McIntosh's Expedition, 1778," ed. by E. G. Williams, *Western Pennsyl-*

vania Magazine, 43 (March-September, 1960), 1-17, 157-177, 267-288.

12. F. B. Heitman, *Historical Register of Officers of the Continental Army During the War of the Revolution*, rev. ed. (Washington, 1914), 371; *Gazette of the State of Georgia*, Feb. 27, 1783, p. 2, col. 2; *Columbian Museum and Savannah Advertiser*, Dec. 6, 1799, p. 3, col. 3, for obituary of William McIntosh.

13. The house numbered 110 East Oglethorpe Avenue in Savannah has for many years been called "the McIntosh house" and has a bronze marker to that effect. This is incorrect. McIntosh's home in Savannah was on the western half of Lot 0, Heathcote Ward facing St. James's (now Telfair) Square. *Travis Abstracts*, Georgia Historical Society.

14. *National Portrait Gallery of Distinguished Americans* (Philadelphia, 1836); Henry Laurens to McIntosh, Sept. 28, 1768, in the C. F. Jenkins Collection, The Historical Society of Pennsylvania, as quoted by A. A. Lawrence in "General Lachlan McIntosh and His Suspension from Continental Command During the Revolution," *G.H.Q.*, XXXVIII (June, 1954), 105-106; William Bartram, *Travels Through North and South Carolina, Georgia, East and West Florida* . . . (London, 1794), 15; *Colls. G.H.S.*, XII (Savannah, 1957), 111, 149; C. C. Jones, *Biographical Sketches of the Delegates from Georgia to the Continental Congress* (Boston, 1891), 139-154; W. J. Northern, ed., *Men of Mark in Georgia*, I (Atlanta, 1907), 246-256.

15. W. J. McIntosh to I. K. Tefft, Dec. 18, 1828, in McIntosh Papers, Folder L-30, Keith Read Collection, University of Georgia Library: "Having been from home for some time I did not reply to your last letter respecting the papers in the hands of Mr. Bevan: The letter which you mentioned, address'd by Genl. Washington, must have been to Genl. Lachlan McIntosh, my Father's Uncle, whose Daughter Mr. Harris married; your letter is not before me, and writing hastily late at night, I cannot answer it properly. I saw Mr. Bevan however recently, who did not appear to like the idea of having his papers disturbed, fearing, probably, some disarrangement among them."

Letters and Documents

1. McIntosh kept his papers folded with a notation as to contents written on a fold. The captions in quotations for the letters and documents in this collection are McIntosh's notations. Unless otherwise noted the papers herein are in McIntosh's hand.

2. Esther and John Cuthbert were the mother and step-father of Sarah Threadcraft. George Threadcraft, her father, probably died about the time he made his will in 1742. No record of the re-marriage of Esther Threadcraft to John Cuthbert has been found.

Despite the promise in this document, John Cuthbert, some thirty years later, changed his mind and made charges against Lachlan McIntosh and George Threadcraft, Jr., for the keep of Sarah and James Threadcraft as children, as shown by the letter below from the Conarroe Papers in the Historical Society of Pennsylvania and here published with the permission of that Society. As a consequence, Lachlan McIntosh and George Threadcraft, Jr., were appointed administrators of the estate of George Threadcraft, Sr. *Gazette of the State of Georgia*, Oct. 5, 1786, p. 3, col. 1; and Apr. 17, 1788, p. 1, cols. 2-3; p. 2, col. 1. There is a certified copy of the will of George Threadcraft, Sr., dated

29 April 1742, in Chatham County Court House, probably obtained by the administrators. With this is a paper in the hand of Lachlan McIntosh, "Remark—on the Inventory" [of George Threadcraft's estate]. The letter referred to follows:

Skidoway Tuesday 11th. July 1786.
Dear George.

This day Week I wrote to you, directed to the care of Mr. Strahacker —requesting you would come down here, as old Mr. Cuthbert is come from Carolina he says to Settle Accounts of your Father's Estate with you & I—the old man is at his Son Seth John's at the orphan House opposite to us—Your Sister contrived to get Sanko (Sancho) from him which brought him over here one day, & set him quite Crazy—he swears Vengeance against us in the Law way immediately—therefore it is absolutely Necessary you should come down immediately to give me every information you can, & to form some plan of our proceedings—if you have a Copy of your Father's will,—Appraisement-Sales—or any other paper or Memorandums respecting the Estate, bring them with you but do not Stay. Your Sister sends Molly with this Letter—& I believe is on a plan of sending her farther, if you Let Sambo go with her, & a written Ticket to prevent their being taken up, from your House & back to you again, upon their way.

I got the particulars of the old Man's Account against yourself & me, before he got Angry,—& he promised to Let me have your Brother Jammies also, but now refuses to do it.

Yr. Sister & the Family Join in Compliments to Mrs. Threatcraft & yourself & am Dear George

Yours Affectionately
[signed] Lachn. McIntosh.

George Threadcraft To John Cuthbert—Dr.
1756. Decr. 15th. To boarding, Clothing, Schooling finding every thing from 15. Decr. 1746 to this date, & Docter's phisick &ca. is 10 yrs. 11 1/2 Months at £ 150 per Year   £ 1645.10.0
To one half of Yr. Brother Jammie's Accot.   570
                                              £ 2215.10

Lachn. McIntosh To John Cuthbert. Dr.
To Boarding, Clothing, Schooling &ca. of Sarah Threadcraft   £ 1350
To Clothes purchased for weding   110
To Dinner at the wedding Cost   50
To new Feather Bed & Blankets   50
To half a Set of Tea Spoons   5
To 7 years hire of Phebe a £ 40   280
To one half Jammie Threadcraft's Accot.   570
                                            £ 2410

Mr. Cuthbert expects to recover Donas, Dolly, Bina, & Mingo, or their Value by these Accounts, and the Interest on them

There were eight known children of Lachlan and Sarah Threadcraft McIntosh. We have made no attempt to find all available information on them. They were:

John, the oldest; died in 1792, never married.
Lachlan, Jr., died 1783; never married.
William (1759-1799); no marriage record found.
George; living at time of father's death in 1806.
Henry Laurens; living at time of father's death in 1806.
Hampden; living at time of father's death. He married Caroline Clifford Nephew and had one son who died young, and two daughters, one of whom married a Winston and the other a Bacon.
Hester (Esther); married (1) John Peter Ward and had a son and a daughter. She married (2) Dr. Nicholas Serle Bayard and had Jane Elizabeth (died 1885) who married the Rev. John Leighton Wilson of South Carolina, and another daughter who married an Eckard.

3. This paper is probably from one of a series appearing in the *Georgia Gazette* and *The South Carolina Gazette* after both papers published the Boston Port Bill on June 8 and June 3, 1774, respectively. They are signed by various pseudonymns. The letter from which this is extracted could not be found in available issues of the two newspapers. The Rev. Haddon Smith, rector at Savannah, is identified as Mercurious, W. W. Manross, comp., *The Fulham Papers in the Lambeth Palace Library* . . . (Oxford, 1965), p. 20.

4. This document, with some differences in words, phrases, capitalization and punctuation is in George White, *Historical Collections of Georgia* (New York, 1854), 554-556, (hereafter cited as White, *Hist. Colls. Ga.*), and A. D. Candler, *The Revolutionary Records of the State of Georgia*, I (Atlanta, 1908). 38-42, (hereafter cited as Candler, *Rev. Recs. Ga.*). White omitted the fifth resolution. This copy, a preliminary draft in McIntosh's hand, is mutilated. The missing portions are supplied in brackets from the previously published copies.

Internal evidence points to McIntosh as the author of these Resolutions; according to White he was the first signer. Some phrases, crossed out in the original, have been retained in this transcription.

5. This letter is pasted on a sheet of paper which covers the name of the addressee. The name was read by holding the paper to the light.

6. Same in White, *Hist. Colls. Ga.*, 90, and Candler, *Rev. Recs. Ga.*, I, 111-112. This paper is in an unknown hand. For McIntosh's letter to George Washington in regard to the affair of the rice ships, see *Colls. G.H.S.*, XII (Savannah, 1957), 1-4.

7. This paper is a preliminary draft of the letter and barely legible. The missing portions have been supplied in brackets from the copy in Peter Force's Transcripts of Georgia Records, Mss. in the Library of Congress.

8. In an unknown hand. See also John Wereat to George Walton, 30 August 1777, *Colls. G.H.S.*, XII, 66-72.

9. In Baker's hand. The letter is mutilated along the edge and missing words or part of words have been supplied in brackets.

10. This account sheet was used as a folder around other papers and bears note: "Accot. against the Public. wth. Vouchers for Visiting the Hospitals in April & May 1778." See "Memorandums 15th. May 1778," above.

11. In an unknown hand. The caption is in McIntosh's hand.

12. In an unknown hand. It is mutilated and incomplete.

13. In the hand of Lachlan McIntosh, Sr. All that can be deciphered of the caption is "Copy ----- from Major McIntosh from Valley forge

March '78." This letter was published in *The Magnolia; or, Southern Appalachian*, New Ser. II (June, 1843), 377.

14. Early in the Revolution the British considered using Russian troops as shown by the following extracts from the Head Quarters Papers: "Earl of Dartmouth to Maj.-Gen. William Howe, 1775, September 5. Whitehall–Secret. That their confident hope of having a large army in America in the spring rests on the ground of an assurrance from the Empress of Russia that she would give any number of infantry that might be wanted, and that a requisition has thereupon been made for twenty thousand men." Same to same "1775, October 27. Whitehall . . . The prospects of troops from Russia doubtful." Historical Manuscripts Commission, *Report on American Manuscripts in the Royal Institution of Great Britain*, I (London, 1904), 7, 17.

15. In an unknown hand.

16. This portion is written on the same sheet as above, though upside down. It may be a separate memorandum. Lack (sometimes Lackie) mentioned in this and other papers was Major Lachlan McIntosh, Jr.

17. In an unknown hand.

18. In Brodhead's hand; title note by McIntosh.

19. Only the salutation and date are in McIntosh's hand.

20. This note, written on a scrap of paper, is barely legible.

21. The order of the Memoranda is not clear. The paper is only partly legible.

22. In the hand of John Irwin. The letter is badly mutilated.

23. In an unknown hand and badly mutilated. Has note on back: "A return of the strength of the Garrisons West of the Mountains January 1st. 1779."

24. In an unknown hand.

25. McIntosh had returned to Georgia at this time, by his own request. He took part in the Siege of Savannah.

26. This is a printed form, filled in by McIntosh. The portions crossed out are crossed out in the original. The title is McIntosh's.

27. Copies of the letters of Glascock and Walton to the Congress referred to in this Declaration are in *Colls. G.H.S.*, XII, 78-80, 115-116. See also the letter of the Continental officers to McIntosh, Jan. 7, 1781, above. The paper is in an unknown hand, but the signatures of the officers are in their own hands.

28. In Cooke's hand, with McIntosh's title.

29. This is a copy in McIntosh's hand and has his note on the back: "Ballingal & Mckinzie, Certificate, of Ben: Andrews.–with Augusta petition." The certificate is not included.

30. See "The Names of Persons in the Georgia Disqualification Act," *Colls. G.H.S.*, XII, 92-96. This list was probably intended to be sent with this letter.

31. In an unknown hand with some notations by McIntosh. Where possible mutilated and blank spaces have been filled in with information from other sources.

32. The date of Cuthbert's commission could not be found. There was a William Johnston of Virginia whose commission as a captain was dated Dec. 24, 1776, and a John Pitt of Virginia who was a Surgeon in the Hospital Department, 1780-1781. F. B. Heitman, *Historical Register of Officers of the Continental Army During the Revolution*, rev. ed. (Washington, 1914), 323, 443. Hereafter cited as Heitman, *Hist. Reg.*

33. This letter, in an unknown hand, from the Continental officers is another refutation of the slander against McIntosh by George Walton and Richard Howley. An account of the examination of these charges is in *Colls. G.H.S.*, XII, 108-118. McIntosh's title of this paper is "Letter to the Officers of Colo. Bland's and Late Colo. Parker's Regt. with their Answer. & Mr. Wereat's Notes. Per Capt. Day." For Wereat's notes, see *ibid.*, 96.

34. In Carleton's hand.

35. A preliminary copy, in McIntosh's hand. It is illegible in places which have been filled in from the copy in Peter Force's Transcripts of Georgia Records, Mss. in the Library of Congress. Compare this with "Letter to Congress on the promotion of General Knox, 1782," *Colls. G.H.S.*, XII, 106-108. An incorrect date, 1779, has been added in a different hand. See also the discussion and votes on the promotions of William Moultrie, James Clinton, Lachlan McIntosh, and Henry Knox, March 1782, in W. C. Ford, ed., *Journals of the Continental Congress, 1774-1789*, XXII (Washington, 1914), 105, 143, 144, 147-148.

36. "Resolved, That such as are in the Continental Service, take rank according to the dates of their Commissions, and the rank they held in the Army at the time of their promotion; and that such as do not hold continental commissions, stand after them in the order in which they are elected." *Ibid.*, 142.

37. There are two copies of this letter in the collection, sent by different vessels. They are in different hands and vary slightly in words, spelling and punctuation, but not in sense. The copy given here, dated April 30, 1782, bears note in McIntosh's hand: "Letter of Menzies Baillie to his Brother Robt. Baillie London 30th April 1782." The other copy, dated May 1782, is incomplete, and has a note in McIntosh's hand: "Menzies Baillie's Letters to his Brother Alexander, dated London May & June 1782." Robert Baillie was Lachlan McIntosh's brother-in-law, and was a Loyalist.

38. In Bedford's hand, with McIntosh's caption. It is mutilated and a section is missing. McIntosh's reply in his own hand is written on the back.

39. This document is not in Journal of the Transactions of Commissioners of Confiscated Estates in Candler, *Rev. Recs. Ga.*, I, 413-607. It is in an unknown hand and badly mutilated. Some words, where the sense seems obvious, have been supplied in brackets.

40. In Wilkinson's hand. This document is in Candler, *Rev. Recs. Ga.*, III, 345-346. A copy of the Memorial, dated 27 June 1783 and in McIntosh's hand, is in the New York Public Library Ms. Miscellaneous Papers. In it he tells of his losses in the war and the hardships his family endured during it.

41. In William McIntosh's hand. There is a copy of this paper in Peter Force's Transcripts of Georgia Records Mss. in the Library of Congress. No account or mention of the horsewhipping of George Walton by William McIntosh and the subsequent courtmartial of William McIntosh has been found in any publication, including contemporary newspapers.

42. From *Gil Blas;* prescribes warm water for every ailment.

43. Preliminary draft; see also *Colls. G.H.S.*, XII, 126-129. This letter is probably in response to a proposal in the House of Assembly to vest in the Governor and Executive Council the powers exercised by the Board of Claims. Candler, *Rev. Recs. Ga.*, III, 471-472.

NOTES   129

44. In the hand of John Wereat.
45. In the hand of John Mackintosh, brother of Lachlan. He retained the Scottish spelling of the name. See also the letter of Charles Scrimsger on this hurricane in *Colls. G.H.S.*, XII 134-135.
46. In Lutterloh's hand; the printed advertisement referred to is not with these papers. Lutterloh was Deputy Quarter Master General of the Continental Army, 1777-1780. Heitman, *Hist. Reg.*, 361.
47. In hand of John Mackintosh. The debt referred to in the letter was discharged; see "Deed Book A Liberty County, p. 63—John McIntosh, Jr. of Liberty County, to John McIntosh, Sr. of St. Thomas, County of Surry, Island of Jamaica. Deed dated Feb. 22, 1786, to secure debt, conveying 12 slaves, made in order to secure the mortgagee as endorser on a note of said John McIntosh, Jr., dated Jan. 30, 1784, payable to Allen & Campbell, Merchants, of Kingston, Jamaica." *Georgia Genealogical Magazine*, No. 15, January 1965, p. 971.
48. The mother of Lachlan and John McIntosh was Margaret Fraser.
49. On the back of this paper is the beginning of another letter by McIntosh: "B———— The time has been, which I must say was the happiest as well as the greatest part of my Life, that I never was perfectly easy out of your Sight, nor altogether happy out of your Company."
50. Lachlan McIntosh's brother-in-law.
51. No record of a marriage of William McIntosh has been found. He died Dec. 1, 1799, aged 40. *Columbian Museum and Savannah Advertiser*, Dec. 6, 1799, p. 3, col. 3.
52. This was the town of McIntosh which shows on some old maps; the town of Oglethorpe, below, is not shown on a map of St. Simons Island, *ca.* 1787, at the Georgia Historical Society.
53. There is nothing on this letter to indicate who wrote it or to whom it was addressed. It is undated.
54. McIntosh's note on the back of this paper: "List of 50. Lottery Tickets United States. 1776. which Colo. Barber is requested to enquire into at Philadelphia, and inform his Humb. Servt. Lachn. McIntosh."
55. In Seagrove's hand.
56. In Denison's hand.
57. This document was published in *G.H.Q.*, III (Sept. 1919), 131-144, under title, "The Case of George McIntosh," by the editor. It apparently belonged to the Georgia Historical Society at that time. It is in an unknown hand, but the caption is in the hand of Lachlan McIntosh.
58. This letter was probably written to Lachlan McIntosh, son of William McIntosh, and not to Gen. Lachlan McIntosh.
59. Written by John Mackintosh, son of Gen. Lachlan McIntosh.
60. This journal is probably in the hand of George McIntosh. He was accused of traitorous correspondence with the enemy and of supplying rice to East Florida. He wrote a "full and true state of the matter" in *The Case of George McIntosh, Esquire, a Member of the Late Council and Convention of the State of Georgia; With the Proceedings Thereon in the Hon. the Assembly and Council of That State* . . . (N.p., 1777).
61. This paper is a fragment. It is not known who wrote it.
62. The three journals of the Siege of Charleston in 1780 which follow—McIntosh's, John Habersham's and an unidentified Subaltern's—were first published, with some modifications, in *The Magnolia; or Southern Appalachian*, New Ser., I (Dec. 1842), 363-374. In that publication the McIntosh and Habersham journals are interspersed with no notations

as to which was which. McIntosh incorporated much of the Habersham journal in his; in a few instances he indicated this by using the initials "J. H." Mutilated places in this copy of the Habersham journal have been filled in, in brackets, from the McIntosh journal. Another copy of John Habersham's journal of the Siege, March 28-May 16, 1780, is in Peter Force's Transcripts of Georgia Records, Mss. in the Library of Congress.

William Moultrie in his *Memoirs of the American Revolution . . .,* II (New York, 1802), 65-85, quoted freely and almost verbatim from the McIntosh and Habersham journals without giving his source. Gen. Moultrie's account continues through May 8, 1780.

The journal of the unidentified Subaltern is probably in his own hand. Most of it is given in footnotes in *The Magnolia,* cited above. It is incorporated in the copy of Habersham's journal in Force's Transcripts. This manuscript is in a very bad condition but it is almost as legible at it was when first published in 1842, for very few words had to be supplied from that copy.

63. The Summons and Gen. Lincoln's answer are in Moultrie, *Memoirs,* 68-70.

64. The Lincoln and Clinton letters and terms of capitulation are in *ibid.,* 73-78, 86-103.

65. Most of Col. Beekman's notes are in a footnote in *The Magnolia,* cited above. Barnard Beekman, Capt. 4th S. C. (Artillery) 14 Nov. 1775; Major, 18 Nov. 1776; Lt.-Col. 24 Oct. 1778; Col. 20 June 1779; taken prisoner at Charleston May 1780; prisoner on parole to close of war. Heitman, *Hist. Reg.,* 96.

Index

Abrahams, Joseph, 80
Abrahams, Levy (Livy), 80
Adventure, ship, 99, 101
Alexander, Gen. William, 46
Allans & Campbell, business deal with John McIntosh, Jr., 66-67, 71-72, 129
Allison, Lt. Henry, 39
Anderson, Maj. Richard C., 44, 45
Andrew, Benjamin, 127
Ansonborough, damaged, 100
Arbuthnot, Adm. Marriott, 99, 106, 114
Aristides, 64
Aristocles, 64
Armour, John, 80
Armstrong, Gen. John, 47
Arnold, Gen. Benedict, 20, 47
Ashley Ferry, 98, 100, 105, 106, 112; River, 110, 113
Augusta, petition of inhabitants, 40-41

Bacon Bridge, 96, 98
Badenoch, Scotland, 4
Baillie, Alexander, 128
Baillie, George, 52
Baillie, James, 52
Baillie, John, 52
Baillie, Menzies, 51-53, 128
Baillie, Robert, 3, 51-53, 128
Baker, Col. John, letter to McIntosh, 17-19; resigns commission, 19; mentioned, 126
Baker, Maj. William (?), 18
Ball, Col. Burgess, 43
Ballard's battery, 106
Ballingal & McKinzie, 127
Barber, Col., 129
Bard, Capt. John, 59
Barge, J., 78
Bartram, William, description of McIntosh, 7
Bayard, Jane Elizabeth, 126

Bayard, Dr. Nicholas Serle, 126
Baylor, Col. George, 98
Beatty, John, 80
Beaufort, S. C., 108
Beaufort Convention, 7
Beaver Creek and town, 32
Bedford, Cpl. Gunning, letter to McIntosh with reply, 53-54; mentioned, 128
Bedford County, Pa., 29
Beecroft, Samuel, 80
Beekman, Col. Barnard, mentioned, 43, 103, 130; notes on siege of Charleston, 112
Ben (slave), 14
Bendix, Isaac (J.), 80
Bennington, Vt., number killed and wounded at, 21
Berrien, John, 19, 25, 26, 27, 28, 81
Bethesda Orphanage, Lachlan and Anne at, 4-5
Betts, John, 80
Bevan, James Vallence, 7-8, 124
Big Plum Creek, 31
Billy (slave), 90
Bing (slave), 125
Bland, Col. Theodorick, 42, 98, 128
Blank, Nicholas, 25
Bloody Marsh, battle of, 3
Board of Claims, letter to Georgia House, 64-65; mentioned, 128
Board of War, 30, 33
Bolton, Robert, 79
Bolton's battery, 99
Bonnie Prince Charlie, 5
Booker, Capt. Gideon, 59
Boston, Mass., brave conduct of people, 10-11; number killed and wounded at, 20
Boston port bill, 126
Boston, ship, 99
Bourke, Thomas, 80
Bowman, Capt. Joshua, 113
Bowyer (Boyer), Col. John, 33

131

Boynton, Joseph, 35
Brahm. See De Brahm
Brandywine, Pa., number killed and wounded at, 21
Brett, Capt., 108
Brick Kilns (Kills) near Savannah, 37
Brickell, John, 79
British, number of troops in America, estimate of killed and wounded, 20-21; number of generals and admirals in America, 48
Brodhead, Daniel, letter to McIntosh, 29-30; mentioned, 33, 127
Brossard, Capt. Celeron, 39, 59
Brown, Ens., 19
Brown, Col. Thomas, in command at Augusta, 40
Brown, William, 80
Brownson, Dr. Nathan, 60, 63
Bryan, Lt. J., 19
Bryan, Jonathan, 95
Buck Bottom fort, 31
Bulloch, James, 79
Bunker Hill, Boston, number of killed and wounded at, 20
Bunkers Hill, Charleston, 98
Burgoyne, Gen. John, 21

Cabell, Col. Samuel, 43
Cadwallader, Gen. John, 47
Callender, Dr., 18
Cambray. See De Cambray
Camden, S. C., 6, 41, 97
Campaign, Lt., 109
Campbell, Col. William (?), 31, 32
Campen, Lt. James, 110
Carleton, Joseph, letter to McIntosh, 45; mentioned, 128
Carlisle, Pa., 33
Cathead Creek, 74
Cattel (Cattle), John, 104
Cecil, Leonard, 80
Cedars, The, Canada, number killed and wounded at, 20
Celeron, Capt. Lewis, 44
Chapman, James, 80
Charles Edward, the Young Pretender, 5
Charleston, S. C., Journals of the siege and capitulation of, 96-122
Cheesborough, John, 25, 28

Cherokee Indians, Hopewell Treaty, 7
Chisholm, Capt. 97
Cincinnati, Georgia Society, McIntosh its first president, 7
Clark, James, 80
Clark, Col. Jonathan, 43, 80
Clark, Col. Thomas, 43
Clarke, William, 80
Clay, Joseph, 79
Clinton, Gen. George, 46
Clinton, Sir Henry, 37, 38, 99, 105, 106, 114, 119, 120, 128, 130
Clinton, Gen. James, 46, 50, 128
Coales, William, 80
Cochran, James, 80
Colleton County, S. C., bounds of parole, 37; McIntosh's plantation in, 38
Collins, Lt. Cornelius, 39
Commissioners of Confiscated Estates, bond from James Habersham for purchase of land, 54-55
Concord, Mass., number killed and wounded at, 20
Connecticut, number of generals, 48
Continental Army, officers captured at Charleston, 43-44; officers and expense of maintenance, 46-48
Continental Army, Georgia Line, officers' opinion of McIntosh, 7; letter respecting commissions of officers, 16-17; declaration of officers respecting McIntosh, 38-40; return of officers, 59; First Regiment commanded by McIntosh, 5
Continental Army, Maryland Line, mentioned, 108
Continental Army, South Carolina, letter respecting officers' rank and pay, 16-17
Continental Army, Virginia Line, officers' endorsement of McIntosh, 42, 45
Continental Congress, 4, 7, 11, 14, 15, 30, 33, 48-50, 108, 111
Conway, Gen. Thomas, 47
Cooke, Robert, letter to McIntosh, 40; mentioned, 127
Cooper River, 100, 101, 102, 103, 105, 107, 108, 109
Cornwallis, Lord Charles, 45, 108

INDEX   133

Coudray (Coudre), Gen. Philip C.
  J.B.T. du, 47
Council of Safety, order to McIntosh, 15
Course, Daniel, 80
Course, Isaac, 80
Courvoisie, Francis, letter from McIntosh, 77
Creek Indians, Galphinton Treaty, 72
Croghan, Maj. William, 44
Crookshanks, Patrick, 90
Currie, John, 80
Cuthbert, Capt. Daniel, 19, 44, 59
Cuthbert, Eleanor Lesesne, marriage agreement, McIntosh to Sarah Threadcraft, 9, 124
Cuthbert, John, 9, 124, 125, 127
Cuthbert, Seth John, 125
Cuyler, Henry, 17, 80

Danbury, Conn., number killed and wounded at, 21
Dandridge, Capt. John, 44
Danzell, Baron, occulist, 71
Darien, Ga., resolutions of committee, 10-14; mentioned, 1, 74, 123
Darien Company, 1
Darien, Isthmus of, 1
Day, Capt. Joseph, 59, 80, 128
De Borre, Gen. Prud'homme, 47
De Brahm, Maj. Ferdinand, 44, 109
De Cambray, Col., 43
De Fermoy, Gen. Matthias A. R., 47
De Haas, Gen. John P., 47
De Kalb, Gen. John, Baron, 47
Delaney, S., 78
Delaplaigne, Capt. Peter Emanuel, 19, 59
Delaroque, James, 80
Delaware, number of Continental generals, 48
Denison, Gideon, letter to McIntosh, 81; mentioned, 129
Deveaux's Swamp, 37
De Woedtke, Gen. Frederick W., Baron, 47
Dillon, Edmond, 80
Dixon, Capt. Tilghman, 44
Doboy Island, town on, 74
Dolly (slave), 125

Donaldson, Andrew, 95
Donas (slave), 125
Doyle, Francis, 80
Ducoines, Lt. John, 63
Du Coudray. See Coudray
Dunbar, Capt. George, 1
Duportail, Gen. Louis Lebique, 43, 46, 48-50, 108, 110
Duval, Capt., 28

Eckard, Mr., 126
Edwards, David, 25
Egmont, John Percival, 1st earl of, 2
Elbert, Col. Samuel, 43, 59
Elfe, Thomas, 80
Essick plantation, 2
Estaing, Charles-Henri, comte d', 51
Ewen, William, 15
Ewing, Nathaniel, 30
Ewing, William, 80

Fenwick's house, burned, 98
Ferguson, Mr., 104
Ferguson's house, 98, 99
Fermoy. See De Fermoy
Ferrell, Adj., killed, 120
Ferrell, Col., ordered to conduct George McIntosh to Philadelphia, 94-95
Fisher, John, 80
Fisher, William Low, 25
Fitzpatrick, Capt. Patrick, 39
Flyming, Thomas, 54-55
Footman, Richard S., 79
Force, Peter, 126, 128
Fort Clinton, number killed and wounded at, 21
Fort Hand, return of troops, 34
Fort Henry, 31, 32, 34
Fort Howe, slaughter near, 18
Fort Johnson, 98, 99, 106, 108, 114
Fort King George, 1
Fort Laurens, 6, 34
Fort McIntosh, 6, 32, 34
Fort Mifflin, number killed and wounded at, 21
Fort Montgomery, number killed and wounded at, 21
Fort Moosa, 2, 4
Fort Morris, 3
Fort Moultrie, number killed and

wounded at, 20; mentioned, 102, 105, 108, 109, 112, 114, 118
Fort Pitt, 22, 25, 30, 31, 33, 34
Fort Quebec, number killed and wounded at, 20
Fort Randolph, 31, 34
Fort Washington, number killed and wounded at, 20
Fraser, Margaret, 129
Fraser, Lt. William, 72
Frazer, Lt. John, 39
Frye, Gen. Joseph, 47
Fuhrer, Maj., 68

Gaddis, Col., 31
Gadsden, Gen. Christopher, 17, 47, 104, 112
Galphinton Treaty, 72
Gates, Gen. Horatio, 46
Geohegan, Ignatius, 80
Georgia, recruiting difficulties, 21; colonial government restored, 42; number of Continental generals, 48; impoverished condition, 82; value of tide lands, 92
Georgia Assembly, mentioned, 4; directs auditor to pay McIntosh's claim, 57-58; letter from Board of Claims, 64-65
Georgia Gazette, 9
Georgia Line. See Continental Army, Georgia Line
Georgia Provincial Congress, 2, 4, 5, 13
German settlers proposed for Georgia, 67-68
Gerrard, Lt. Charles, 111
Gibbes's (Gibbs's), 98, 99, 113; battery, 105
Gibbie, Mr., 66, 67
Gibson, Col. John, 25, 31
Gilbank, Capt. John, killed, 99
Gillies, Alexander, 52
Gillison, Capt. John, 44
Gilmore, Thomas, 25, 27
Gist, Gen. Mordecai, 46
Gist, Col. Nathaniel, 43
Glascock, Lt. Thomas, 19, 39, 59
Glascock, William, letter rsepecting McIntosh quoted, 38; refuted, 42, 55; mentioned, 127
Glascow (slave), 14

Glover, Gen. John, 46
Goodwin, Capt. Uriah, 109
Graham, John, 55
Great Bridge, Va., number killed and wounded at, 20
Great Britain, proposal to recover claims against, 67-68
Green, Gen. Nathanael, 46
Grieve, Capt., 71
Grimke, Col. John F., 43
Gwinnett, Button, duel with McIntosh, 5; charges of adherents against McIntosh mentioned, 7

Habersham, James, 54, 55, 64, 80
Habersham, John, mentioned, 18, 44, 59, 80, 129, 130; journal of the siege of Charleston, 108, 109, 113-115
Habersham, Joseph, letter from L. McIntosh, Jr., 21, 23-24; mentioned, 79, 97
Haddrells (Haddrills) Point, 40, 41, 107, 108
Hall, Ens., 110
Hall, J., 80
Hall, Maj., 107
Hall, Mrs. Nathaniel, 71
Hampstead Hill, 114
Hand, Gen. Edward, 46
Handley (Hendley), Capt. George, 19, 39, 59
Hardings, Commodore, 20
Harlem, N. Y., number killed and wounded at, 20
Harleston, Maj. Isaac, 44
Harney, Col. Selby, 43
Harrington, Col. Henry William, 114
Harris, Charles, 124
Harris, Maj., 107
Hays, Lt. Arthur, 39
Hazen, Gen. Moses, 46
Heath, Gen. William, 43, 46, 112
Hell Gate Bridge, N. Y., number killed and wounded at, 20
Henderson, Col. William, 43, 107, 117
Henry, Mr., 29
Henry, Gov. Patrick, 31
Hero, ship, 51
Herriott, James, 55

INDEX

Hervey's, 98
Hessian troops, 122. See also Yagers
Heth, Capt. Henry, 31
Heth, Col. William, 112
Hicks, Capt. Isaac, 59
Hides, methods of procuring, 30-31
Hill, Capt. Bayler, 44, 45, 101
Hillary, Lt. Christopher, 39
Hobcaw, 106, 109, 110; Neck, 102, 103
Hodgson, William B., 123
Hogg, Lt. Sam, 45
Hogg, Maj. Thomas, 44, 80, 102, 108
Hogg Island, 109
Hogun, Gen. James, 43, 47, 98, 99
Hollydays Cove, return of troops, 34
Holmes, John, 73
Hopewell Treaty, 7
Hopkins, Col. Samuel, 43, 45, 97, 121
Horry, Col. Daniel, 98
Houstoun, Ann Priscilla, married George McIntosh, 4
Houstoun, George, letter from McIntosh, 14
Houstoun, Sir George, action against William and Lachlan McIntosh, 86-87
Houstoun, James, administrator of George McIntosh's estate, 84-85, 91
Houstoun, John, action against William and Lachlan McIntosh, 86; appointed Superior Court judge, subscription in favor of, 79-80; mentioned, 100
Houstoun, Sir Patrick, mentioned, 4; administrator of George McIntosh's estate, 84-85, 87
Howe, Gen. Robert, 23, 46
Howe, Gen. William, 23, 127
Howell, Capt. John, 77
Howley, Richard, 128
Huger, Gen. Isaac, 46, 96, 97, 98, 102
Hunter, Capt., 93
Huntington, Gen. Jedidiah, 46
Hurricane in Jamaica described, 65-66
Hutson, Mr., 104
Hyrne, Maj. Edmund, wounded, 113

Indian Doctor, 14

Indian troubles, 86, 89, 90
Iron Hill, Newcastle County, Del., number killed and wounded at, 21
Irvine, Dr., 67
Irvine, Gen. James, 46
Irwin, John, letter to McIntosh, 32-33; mentioned, 127

Jackson, Charles, 80
Jackson, Ebenezer, 80
Jackson, James, 79, 89
James Island, 98, 101, 109; battery, 102
Johns Island, 96
Johnson, Lt. Laban, 39
Johnson, Capt. William, 44
Johnston, Matthew, 80
Johnston, Mr., 33
Johnston, William, 127
Jones, Seaborn, 63
Jordan, Lt. William, 39

Kershaw, Col. Joseph, 97
Kincaid (Kincade), George, 87
Kiskaminatis Creek, 31
Kittaning, 31
Knox, Gen. Henry, mentioned, 46, 128; letter regarding promotion of, 48-50

Lafayette, Marquis de, 46
Lafitte, Peter, 80
Lamb, William, 80
Lampriers (Lempriers) Point, 102, 103, 106, 107, 108, 109, 115, 117, 118, 119, 121
Lancaster, Pa., 29, 33, 35
Lane, Joseph, 24, 59
Langworthy, Edward, 15
Lartezette, Mr., 96
Laumoy (Lamoy, Lemoy) ...., de Mons, 43, 103, 104, 105, 111, 112
Laurens, Henry, 5, 6, 124
Laurens, Col. John, 25, 106, 107, 113
Lavein (Lieven), P.D. & Co., 80
Leach (Leatch), Benjamin, 80
Leake, Richard, 88
Learned, Gen. Ebenezer, 47
Le Conte, William, 97
Lee, Gen. Charles, letter from McIntosh, 16-17; date of promotion, 47

Legge, William, 2d Earl of Dartmouth, 127
Leggett, Abraham, 80
Leslie, Gen. Alexander, 121, 122
Lewis, Gen. Andrew, 47
Lewis, Bessie, 8
Lewis, Maj. William, 44
Lexington, Mass., number killed and wounded at, 20
Lillington, Gen. John Alexander, 112
Lincoln, Gen. Benjamin, 37, 46, 96, 98, 99, 100, 101, 102, 103, 104, 105, 106, 107, 110, 111, 112, 114, 120, 130
Lindsey, Benjamin, 80
Little Plum Creek, 31
Lloyd, Benjamin, 63, 79
Lockhart, Samuel (?), 31
Long Island, number killed and wounded at, 20
Lord, Peter, killed, 111, 118
Lord George Germaine, ship, 108
Lottery. See U. S. Lottery
Love, John, 80
Lowe, Maj. Philip, 44, 59, 109
Lowndes, Mr., 99
Lucas, Capt. John, 39, 59
Lucena (Lucenia), Lucas, 80
Lutterloh, Emanuel, letter to McIntosh, 67-68; mentioned, 129
Lytle, Col. Archibald, 43, 112

McAllister, Matthew, 80, 91
McCord, Mrs., 97
McCormick, Mr., 97
McCredie, Andrew, 80
McCulloch, Mary, 74
McDaniel, Lt. William, 39
McDougall, Gen. Alexander, 46
McGillivray, James, 80
McGillivray, Lachlan, house on Savannah River mentioned, 37
McIntosh, Anne, 2, 3, 4-5
McIntosh, Dr., 72
McIntosh, George (brother of Lachlan), mentioned, 2; sketch of, 3-4, 82-84; bill in equity re estate of, 81-91; account of arrest and journey to Philadelphia, 94-95; case of, 129
McIntosh, George (son of Lachlan), 126
McIntosh, Hampden, 126
McIntosh, Henry Laurens, 126
McIntosh, Hester (Esther), 126
McIntosh, Janet, 2
McIntosh (Mackintosh), John (brother of Lachlan), mentioned, 2, 129; sketch, 3; letters to Lachlan, 65-67, 71-72
McIntosh, John (son of Lachlan), mentioned, 6, 79, 93, 126, 129; questionable business venture, 66-67, 71-72
McIntosh, John (son of William), 3, 39, 59
McIntosh, John Houstoun, mentioned, 4; complainant vs William and Lachlan McIntosh, 81-91
McIntosh, John Mor, sketch, 2; mentioned, 123
McIntosh, Gen. Lachlan, mentioned, 2, 3, 32, 94, 114, 126; sketch, 4-7; duel with Gwinnett mentioned, 5; marriage and settlement, 5, 9, 124-125; letters from, 14, 16-17, 30, 37, 41-42, 48-50, 54, 77, 124-125; letters to, 17-19, 29-30, 32-33, 40, 45, 53, 65-68, 71-72, 81; order from Council of Safety, 15; petition to Georgia House, 17; expense accounts, 19-20, 24-25, 33, 35, 36-37, 68-70, 72; pay as Brig-Gen., 35; parole, 37-38; plantation in Colleton, S. C., 38; declaration of Georgia officers respecting, 38-40; endorsement by Virginia officers, 42, 45; dates of commissions, 43, 46; auditor directed to pay claims, 57-58; behavior of Walton toward, 63; president of Board of Claims, 64; deed of gift to son William, 73-76; list of lottery tickets, 77-78; answer to bill in equity of J. H. McIntosh, 81-91; in Charleston for several years, 82; losses due to war, 85; prisoner, exchanged for Gen. O'Hara, 85; journal of siege of Charleston, 96-112; takes family to South Carolina, 96-97; ordered to command S. C. militia, 98; on capitulation of Charleston, 101, 105;

INDEX

home in Savannah, 124; promotion, 128
McIntosh, Lachlan, naval officer at Savannah, 91
McIntosh, Lachlan (son of Lachlan), sketch, 6; letter to Joseph Habersham, 21, 23-24; mentioned, 19, 25, 41, 65, 89, 97, 126, 127
McIntosh, Lachlan (son of William), 19, 59, 129
McIntosh, Lewis, 2, 123
McIntosh, Margaret, 2
McIntosh, Phineas, 2, 123
McIntosh, Sarah (wife of Lachlan), letter from McIntosh, 41-42
McIntosh, W. J., 124
McIntosh, William (brother of Lachlan), sketch, 2-3; mentioned, 4, 5, 18, 124; defendant in bill of equity, estate of George McIntosh, 81-91
McIntosh, William (son of Lachlan), sketch, 6; mentioned, 8, 19, 39, 58, 59, 126, 128, 129; declares Walton a coward and a villain, 58; defense for horsewhipping Walton, 58, 60-63; settlement of account, 65; deed of gift from father, 73-76; questionable purchase of Negroes of estate of George McIntosh, 87-89
McIntosh, town of, 129
McIver, John, 80
McIver, Mr., 51
Mackay, Hugh, 1
McKee, Capt. Griffith John, 44
MacKenzie, William, letters on Scots settlers, 1, 2, 123
Mackintosh, Alexander, 123
McLean, John, 66, 67
McLeod, Donald, 80
McQueen, Alexander, 80
McQueen, John, 96
Malmedy (Malmady), Col. Francis, Marquis de, 102, 108, 109, 110, 116, 118; death, 119
Manson, Duncan, 79
Martin, Gov. John, 54, 65
Martin, Mr., 96, 98
Maryland, number of Continental generals, 48

Massachusetts, number of Continental generals, 48
Matthews, Capt., 112
Matthews, William, 39
Maxwell, Gen. William, 21, 47, 63
Meanley, Lt. John, 39
Mebane, Col. Robert, 43
Melven (Melvin), Capt. George, 39, 44, 59
Mercer, Gen. Hugh, 47
Mercurious, letter to newspaper, 9-10, 126
Meriwether, Lt. David, 45
Mifflin, Gen. Thomas, 47
Miller, Capt. Elisha, 39
Milton, John, 19, 59
Mingo, (slave), 125
Minis, Mrs. Abraham, 98
Minis, Philip, 84
Mirrilies, James, 80
Mitchell, David, 80
Mitchell, Maj. Ephraim, 44
Mitchell, Capt. William (?), 112
Mohichon, 32
Molly (slave), 125
Moncks (Monks) Corner, 96, 101, 102
Monongahela, 31
Montaigut, David, 79
Montgomery, Gen. Richard, 47
Moore, Gen. James, 47
Moore, John, 80
Moore, William, 80
Morgan, 31
Morgan, Gen. Daniel, 46
Morison, Mr., 66, 67
Morristown, N. J., 108
Moseley, Capt. William, 44
Mosely, Lt. Littleberry, 59
Mossman, James, 80
Moultrie, Capt. Thomas, killed, 107, 118
Moultrie, Gen. William, mentioned, 17, 43, 46, 98, 100, 102, 103, 105, 112, 128, 130; letter to Congress on promotion of officers, 48-50
Mount Pleasant, S. C., captured by Cornwallis, 108
Muhlenberg, Gen. Peter, 46
Mumford, Capt. Joseph, 111
Munroe, John, 73

Murfree (Murphree), Maj. Hardy, 25
Muskingum River, 32, 95

Nash, Capt. Clement, 41, 42, 94, 95, 99
Nelson, Maj. John, 44
Netherclift, Thomas, 80
Netherland (Neatherland), Lt., 19
Neville, Col. John, 36, 43
Neville, Col. Presley, 102
New Hampshire, number of Continental generals, 48
New Inverness, Ga., 1
New Jersey, mentioned, 21, 35; number of Continental generals, 48
New York, number killed and wounded at, 20; number of Continental generals, 48; reinforcements from, 107, 110
Neyle, Philip, killed, 102
Nixon, Gen. John, 47
Norfolk, Va., number killed and wounded at, 20
North Carolina, difficulties of recruiting in, 21; number of Continental generals, 48
Northumberland County, Pa., 29

Oates' plantation, 37
Odingsells, Charles, 79
Oglethorpe, James Edward, 1, 2, 3, 5
Oglethorpe, town on St. Simons Island, 74, 129
O'Hara, Gen. Charles, exchanged for McIntosh, 85
Owens, Owen, 80

Parker, Capt. Alexander, 45
Parker, George, 80
Parker, Col. Richard, mentioned, 42, 107, 112, 128; killed 108, 118
Parker, Lt. Thomas, 45
Parkman, William, 80
Patton, Col. John, 25, 43, 46
Payne, Mr., 97
Payne, Capt. Tarlton, 45
Pearre, Lt. Nathaniel, 39
Pelham, Maj. Charles, 44
Pendleton, Nathaniel, 81

Pennsylvania, number of Continental generals, 48; cost of government, 57
Peyton, Capt. Valentine, killed, 120
Phebe (slave), 125
Phillips, Lt. Samuel, killed, 110, 118
Pinckney, Charles Cotesworth, mentioned, 43, 107, 112, 118; on capitulation of Charleston, 104-105
Pinckney, Maj. Thomas, 44, 109
Pinder, William, 80
Pitt, Capt. John, 44, 127
Pittsburg, Pa., 35
Pockety Creek, 31
Point tract, 74
Pollock, Coshman (Coachman), 80
Pollock, James, 33
Polly (slave), 89, 90
Pomeroy, Gen. Seth, 47
Poor, Gen. Enoch, 47
Prevost, Gen. Augustin, 6
Prince of Wales, ship, 1
Princeton, N. J., number killed and wounded at, 20
Prisoners of war, list of officers captured at Charleston, 42-44
Proctor (Procktor), Col. Thomas, 31
Providence, ship, 99
Pulaski, Gen. Casimir, 47, 98, 102
Putnam, Benjamin, 80
Putnam, Henry, 80
Putnam, Gen. Israel, 46

Quebec, number killed and wounded at, 20
Queen of France, ship, 99
Quit rent laws, 11, 12

Ramsay, Dr. David, 104
Randons Bottom, return of troops, 34
Ranger, ship, 99, 101
Read, Gen. James, 47
Reading Road, number killed and wounded at, 21
Recruiting, difficulties of, 21, 23
Redbank, N. J., number killed and wounded at, 21
Reed, Gen. Joseph, 47
Rees, David, 39

INDEX

Regiment of Horse, complaints against, 18, 19
Rennie (Reny), William, 80
Rhode Island, number of Continental generals, 48
Rice, Capt., 25
Rice lands, value of in Georgia 92
Rice vessels, resolutions of Council of Safety regarding, 15
Richardson, Capt., 97
Roberts, Joseph, 80
Robertson, James, 103
Robertson, John, 80
Roche, Lt. Matthew, 19
Roliter, Capt., 31
Rozier, Jordan, 25
Russell, Col. Williams, 43, 118
Russian troops, attempt of British to secure, 23, 127
Rutledge, Edward, 119
Rutledge, Gov. John, 100, 101, 110

Sabb, Thomas, 96, 98
St. Augustine, 2
St. Clair, Gen. Arthur, 46
St. Clair, Lord, wounded, 113
St. Johns, N.B., number killed and wounded at, 20
Salisbury, N. C., 41, 42
Salter, Capt., 17, 19
Sambo (slave), 125
Sancho (slave), 125
Sandusky, Ohio, 32
Sangrado, Dr., 62
Sarzedas (Surzedas), Lt. David, 19
Savannah, Siege of, 6; McIntosh's orders to Col. Twiggs, 37
Schuyler, Gen. Philip, 47
Scott, Gen. Charles, 43, 46, 103, 117
Scott, Capt. William (?), 94
Scott, Col. William, 108, 118
Screven, Col. James, 18
Scrimger, Lt., 19
Scrimsger, Charles, 129
Seagrove, James, letter to John McIntosh, 79; mentioned, 80, 129
Shaffer, Balthazar, 80
Sheftall, Benjamin, Sr., 80
Sheftall, Mordecai, opinion of McIntosh, 7
Shelton, Capt. Clough, 44
Shingle Creek, 74

Simons, Col. Maurice, 103
Simpson, James, 80
Simpson, John & Co., 14
Simpson, Mr., 51
Slavery, opposed by Darien committee, 13
Smallwood, Gen. William, 46, 50
Smith, Rev. Haddon, 126
Smith, John, 80
Smith, Capt. John C., 44
Smith, Lt. Col., 111
Smithson, F. T., 80
South Carolina, number of Continental generals, 48
Southern states, critical situation of, 76-77
Spalding, Thomas, 5
Spencer, Gen. Joseph, 47
Spiers, McLeod & Co., 79
Stakes, George, 33
Stark, Gen. John, 46
Staten Island, number killed and wounded at, 21
Steele, Col. Archibald (?), 31
Steele, John, 91
Stephens, Gen. Adam, 47
Stephens, William, 2, 80, 86
Stephenson (Stevenson), Maj. David, 44, 117
Steuben, Gen. Frederick W. A., Baron von, 6, 46
Stewart, Ann, 86
Stewart, Lt., 63
Stiles, Capt., 109
Stirk, Samuel, 80, 86
Stirling, Earl of. See Alexander, William
Storie, John, 80
Strohacker (Strahacker), Mr., 125
Stubblefield, Lt. Beverly, 45
Sullivan, Daniel, 80
Sullivan, Gen. John, 21, 47
Sumner, Gen. Jethro, 46
Sumter, Col. Thomas, 96

Taliaferro, Capt. Benjamin, 45
Tarleton, Col. Banastre, 103
Taylor, J., 80
Tebzum, Thomas, letter to John McIntosh, 93
Tefft, Israel Keech, 124
Telfair, Edward, 97

Templeton, Capt. Andrew, wounded, 110; died, 118
Tennill, Lt. Francis, 39, 59
Ternant, Col. John Baptiste, 106
Theus, Capt. Simeon, 102
Thomas, Gen. John, 47
Thomson, 25
Thomson, Gen. William, 47
Threadcraft, Esther Lesesne, 5
Threadcraft, George, Jr., party to deed, 73-76; letter from McIntosh, 124-125
Threadcraft, George, Sr., 5, 124
Threadcraft, James, 124, 125
Threadcraft, Sarah, marriage to Lachlan McIntosh, 5, 9, 124-125
Throop, George, 80
Ticonderoga, number killed and wounded at, 20
Tinning, Col., 106
Transports, British, number of prisoners taken in, 20
Tredway, Dr. George, 68
Trenton, N. J., number killed and wounded at, 20
Truite, ship, 99
Tuckeseking, 55
Tunno, John, 51
Tuscarawas Town, 96
Twiggs, Col. John, orders from McIntosh, 37

U. S. civil officers, estimate of number and pay, 56-57
U. S. lottery, 77-78
U. S. military establishment, estimate of number of officers and pay, 57

Valk, Jacob, 4
Valley Forge, Pa., 5, 21, 26-28, 30, 67
Vanderlocht, William, 80
Vanmitter, 31
Varnum, Gen. James M., 47
Vernie, Maj. Peter J. F., killed, 102
Vessels forbidden to leave Savannah, 15
Vigilant, ship, 108
Virginia, difficulty of recruiting in, 21, 23; number of Continental generals, 48
von Steuben. See Steuben

Waggener, Maj. Andrew, 44
Wagnon, Lt. John Peter, 39
Wall, Richard, 80
Wallace, Col. Gustavus B., 43
Wallace, John, 80
Walsh, Capt. Patrick, 59
Walton, George, mentioned, 8, 19, 127, 128; letter to Congress refuted, 38, 42, 45; declared a coward and a villain, 58; horsewhipped by William McIntosh, Jr., 58, 60-63
Walton, Lt. Jesse, 19, 39
Wando Neck, 105; River, 102, 103
Wappetaw, 103; Bridge, 106, 115; Creek, 100, 106, 111
Wappoo Cut, 98; Neck, 98, 113, 114, 115
Ward, Gen. Artemus, 47
Ward, John Peter, 80, 126
Warley, Capt. Felix, 44
Washington, George, 5, 46, 108, 124
Watlington, Francis, 80
Watt, Alexander, 80
Wayne, Gen. Anthony, 46
Webster, Col. James, 103, 116
Weedon, Gen. George, 46, 49
Welch, Mr., 71
Wereat, John, 17, 65, 126, 128, 129
Western Department, commanded by McIntosh, 5; mentioned, 6
Western expedition, 29, 30-32, 33-34
Whitcomb (Whitecome), John, 47
White Plains, N. Y., number killed and wounded at, 20
Whitefield, George, 4
Whitefield, James, 80
Wilkinson, Gen. James, 47
Wilkinson, John, 58, 128
Wilkinson, Morton, 97
Williams, Capt. Benjamin, 25
Williamsburg, S. C., 5, 9
Williamson, John G., 80
Wilson, G., 80
Wilson, Capt. James (?), 112
Wilson, John Leighton, 126
Woedtke. See De Woedtke
Woodford, Gen. William, 43, 47, 99, 114, 117
Woodhouse, Robert, 80
Wooster, Gen. David, 47
Worsham, Lt. Richard, 118

Wreck, John, 80
Wright, Edward, 80
Wright, Sir James, petition from Augusta citizens, 40-41
Wright, Capt. Shadrack, 19
Yagers (Yagres), Hessian corps, 118
York, Pa., 29, 30, 33

CPSIA information can be obtained
at www.ICGtesting.com
Printed in the USA
LVHW092030161021
700652LV00006B/175